THE MOTHER WOUND

A Love Story Told In Blood

PIA PHILLIPS

This book is a work of creative nonfiction. Certain names, identifying details, and circumstances have been altered to protect privacy. Any resemblance to actual persons, living or dead, is coincidental except where explicitly stated.

The reflections, spiritual interpretations, and experiences expressed in this book represent the author's perspective and are not intended as medical, psychological, legal, or therapeutic advice.

For speaking engagements, workshops, appearances, and bulk orders: info@thesoulspaonline.com.

ISBN: 979-8-234-00606-6
Paperback Edition

Library of Congress Control Number: 2026905663

Published by: The SOUL Spa LLC | Marietta, GA

Printed in the United States of America

DEDICATION

For my grandmother—
who protected me when I needed it most and showed me the difference between blood and belonging.
I love you.

PROLOGUE
The Cards Don't Lie

They tell you to forgive.

They tell you she did her best.

They tell you—these soft-voiced women draped in white linen and copper jewelry—that you chose your mother before you were born. That your soul signed some sacred contract in the dark between stars. That every wound was agreed upon in advance. A lesson. A blessing in disguise.

But they never tell you what to do when she shows up in every lifetime holding the same knife.

I laid the cards out at 3 a.m., when truth is less polite. When the veil thins and the lies we rehearse during daylight lose their grip. Tarot first. Then oracle cards. Then the cowrie shells my grandmother—my other mother—pressed into my palm before she died.

"Some blood protects," she whispered. Some blood poisons. Learn the difference.

The question I asked was simple:

What am I missing?

What answered me was not a vision. It was a memory with sharp teeth.

Not one lifetime—*many.*

She has worn crowns and aprons. Silk and iron. She has come to me as mother, sister, midwife, matron, caretaker—always familiar, always trusted, always close enough to touch… and close enough to complete the work.

I saw myself as a daughter used for labor, my cries absorbed by fields that never answered. I saw her there too—not always with warmth, sometimes with silence, sometimes with a smile that said, *this is just the way things are.*

I saw New Orleans, gaslight, and velvet. A brothel thick with perfume and secrets. I was the madam's daughter—raised among men who bought women by the hour—and she taught me early what my body was worth. Taught me how love is bartered. How protection always comes at a cost.

I saw myself split in the womb.

Two heartbeats. Me and my brother.

A choice made before breath.

She wanted the boy. Only the boy.

I lived. He did not.

And even then—even *there*—I carried the weight of being the wrong survivor. Loved and resented in the same breath. Fed with one hand, starved with the other.

There were other lives. Some sharp. Some slow. Some dressed up as care. Some dressed up as destiny.

Different eras. Different names. Same wound.

And now, this life—this mother.

The spiritual world wants to call it karma. They want incense and affirmations. They want forgiveness before truth. They want you small and grateful and quiet about the ways you were cut.

They want you to say, I chose her, and leave it there.

But what if choosing the lesson doesn't mean consenting to the abuse?

What if the contract was never about suffering—but about seeing?

What if the wound doesn't ask for forgiveness at all—what if it demands recognition?

No one talks about the daughters who trace the bloodline backward instead of transcending it. The women who stop performing healing and start demanding answers. The ones who finally say the unspeakable thing out loud—

You were not my greatest teacher. You were the thing I survived.

And survival is not the same as freedom.

This is not a book about shaming mothers. This is a book about telling the truth—when love was used as a leash.

About the unseen forces that move through bloodlines—not attachments, but agreements made in terror, sacrifices mistaken for love, and wounds that learned how to survive by repeating themselves and calling it fate.

My story is not unique. That is the problem.

The cards are still on the altar. One appears every time, no matter how I shuffle or cut the deck. No matter how I ask.

The Tower.

Lightning splitting stone. Foundations collapsing. Everything built to keep the secret finally giving way.

Here is what they don't tell you about The Tower:

Sometimes you are not the one falling. Sometimes you are the lightning.

Turn the page if you are done being told to forgive before you are allowed to understand.

Turn the page if you are ready to look at inheritance without illusion.

Turn the page if you know that some stories do not end in light—they end in fire. And fire, when held consciously, does not destroy—

It tells the truth.

CHAPTER 1
What the Body Never Forgot

I was raised by my grandmother, but I was *waiting* for my mother.

Waiting has a sound to it. It hums in the background of your childhood like an appliance you can't turn off. It sounds like tires on gravel that never quite reach the driveway. Like the doorbell that doesn't ring. Like your name being said halfway, as if someone might finish calling it and then…doesn't.

My grandmother's house smelled like hot grease, Zest soap, and old wood that had survived too many winters. It was a house that knew how to hold people. The walls were thick. The furniture was heavy. Nothing fragile survived there long—not objects, not emotions. She believed in structure. In routine. In keeping a child fed, clothed, and alive.

She loved me the way women love when love has already cost them something.

But love, even good love, doesn't cancel longing. And I longed for my mother the way children do—without language, without strategy, without protection.

I knew her first as an idea.

An absence with a face.

"She's coming to visit," my grandmother would say, not looking at me when she said it.

Those words would light something feral in my chest.

This time, I thought.

This time she'll stay.

I would rehearse it in my body. What I'd pack. What toys I'd bring. Whether I'd finally get to sleep in a house where my mother's things lived. I didn't imagine perfection. Children rarely do. I just imagined *belonging*.

When she arrived, the air changed.

My grandmother's shoulders stiffened. Her mouth tightened in a way that told me she had already traveled this road and didn't expect a different destination. The house, which had always felt solid, suddenly felt crowded—like two histories were standing too close together.

My mother came in carrying perfume and impatience. Lipstick too red for daytime. Eyes that looked through rooms instead of at them. She hugged me the way people hug when they're performing care, not feeling it—quick, practiced, already halfway gone.

And yet—

My body leaned toward her anyway.

That's the thing nobody warns you about. The body doesn't listen to the story you tell yourself. It responds to blood. To pattern. To memory older than words.

I watched her constantly when she visited. The way she moved. The way she spoke to other adults but not to me. I studied her like there would be a test later and this time I planned to pass.

At night, I lay awake listening for conversations through walls. Adult voices, low and careful. My name said like a liability.

"She can't—"

"It's not the right time—"

"You know I'm not—"

The sentences never finished. They didn't have to.

Morning always came too fast. Visits ended the way they began—abruptly. No ceremony. No explanation that made sense to a child whose bags were already packed in her imagination.

I would stand in the doorway and watch her leave.

Every time, some part of me believed this was the moment she'd turn around. That realization would hit her mid-step. That she'd look at me—not past me, and say, *"Come on girl, get your things. You're coming with me."*

She never did.

The rejection wasn't loud. It didn't announce itself. It settled in quietly, the way dampness does—seeping into places no one checks until the black mold shows.

My grandmother never chased her down the steps. Never begged. Never explained.

Later, much later, I would understand why.

She had already been that girl.

The daughter who waited.

The daughter who hoped.

The daughter who learned too early that mothers can be physically present and still unreachable.

She didn't name it for me because no one had named it for her. But she protected me the only way she knew how—by teaching me how to survive disappointment without falling apart in public.

"Don't go empty," she once said, watching me stare out the

window long after my mother's cab was gone. "Some people do that. They leave their bodies when love doesn't come."

I didn't know what she meant then.

But my body did.

My body remembered what my mind was still too young to name. I had been empty once. At the very beginning. In those first hours after birth when a baby is supposed to be held, skin to skin, when the neural pathways for love and safety are wired through touch.

I was alone.

Not with her.

The nurses must have held me. My grandmother came as fast as she could. But in that space between being born and being claimed, something in me learned to wait. Learned that love was conditional. Learned that my own mother could look at me and choose distance.

That night, I dreamed of a house burning from the inside out. No flames visible. Just heat. Pressure. Walls holding too much history.

I woke up with my heart racing, a sensation I would come to recognize over lifetimes—the warning bell that rings when a memory is waking up.

This was not the first time she had left me. And something ancient in me knew it would not be the last.

I didn't know then that the dream wasn't a dream at all. The fire had already happened. And the woman who left me standing in the smoke wore my mother's eyes—borrowed from another lifetime, another sky.

CHAPTER 2
The First Betrayal (Egypt)

I'd heard people talk about past lives, but I didn't know they were an actual thing until I couldn't ignore them anymore.

The dreams came first. Not the hazy, forgettable kind that dissolve with morning light, but the ones that leave residue—taste, temperature, terror. The ones where you wake up knowing things you have no reason to know.

I dreamed of sand. Endless. The kind that gets into everything—your mouth, your hair, the folds of fabric you can't name but somehow remember wearing.

I dreamed of a room with stone walls.

Cool.

Dark.

The smell of oil lamps and something medicinal I couldn't place.

And I dreamed of her.

Not my mother as she is now, but the energy of her. The signature. Like a song played in a different key but still unmistakably the same melody.

The hypnotherapy session wasn't my idea.

A friend—one of those women who collects modalities like charms on a bracelet—had been insisting for months. "You need to do a past life regression. I'm serious. There's something you're not seeing. Trust me. It will help you get to the bottom of this."

I resisted. Not because I didn't believe, but because I suspected if I looked, I'd find something I couldn't un-find.

But the dreams wouldn't stop. And the feeling—that feeling, the one that lived in my chest like a rock I'd swallowed lifetimes ago—kept growing heavier.

So, I went.

The hypnotherapist's office smelled like sandalwood and old books. She was older, melanated, calm, the kind of woman who'd seen enough souls bare themselves that nothing surprised her anymore.

Her name was Pamela Michaels, though she told me to call her Pam.

"Tell me what brought you here," she said, settling into the chair across from me.

I told her about the dreams. The feeling in my chest. The sense that something was wrong, not just in this life, but deeper. Older.

"And your mother?" she asked gently.

I hesitated. "She...we don't have a close relationship. She abandoned me when I was born. My grandmother raised me."

Pam nodded, no judgment in her face. "And the feeling in your chest—can you describe it?"

I pressed my hand to my heart. "It's heavy. Like I'm carrying something that doesn't belong to me. Like grief, but I don't know what I'm grieving."

"Okay," she said. "Get comfortable on the couch. Let's see what your soul wants to show you."

She guided me into a light trance—breathing, relaxation, letting my conscious mind step aside so something deeper could surface.

"I want you to go back," she said, voice low and rhythmic. "Not to your childhood. Go further. To the lifetime that holds the key to what you're carrying now. The original wound. Let your soul show you where this injury began."

My breathing slowed. The room fell away.

And then—

I wasn't on the couch anymore.

The Nile Delta. 1320 BCE.

I am twelve years old, though I don't know it in those terms. Time is measured differently here—by floods, by harvests, by the phases of the moon.

My name is Nefret. It means "beautiful."

I am a daughter of the temple. Not nobility, but not common either. My mother—she is here, I know her instantly even though her face is different—is a priestess. Respected. Feared, even. She serves Sekhmet, the lioness goddess, the one who devours and destroys.

She is powerful in ways I am not.

And I am her disappointment.

I know this the way I knew it in this life as a little girl—in my grandmother's house, watching my mother's cab pull away. The body remembers rejection across centuries. It doesn't need the same words. It recognizes the posture. The turning away. The coldness that lives behind eyes that should hold warmth.

In this life, she wanted a son.

She got me instead.

"How does that make you feel?" Pam asked.

Unwanted.

I can feel it in every interaction—the way she looks at me as if I am proof of some cosmic error. A waste of a womb. A girl-child when she prayed for a boy who could carry power, lineage, legacy.

I try. Gods, I try.

I memorize the chants. I learn the sacred texts. I perfect the rituals, hoping that competence might become love if I just work hard enough.

She notices. But she does not soften.

"You are *adequate,*" she tells me once, and the word lands like a brick.

Not gifted. Not chosen. Adequate—mediocre.

There is a fever that comes through the temple that year.

People fall ill quickly—burning, delirious, crying out to gods who seem far away. The other priestesses work tirelessly, brewing remedies, laying cool cloths on foreheads, whispering prayers over the dying.

I fall sick on the third day.

I remember the heat. The way my body felt like it was being consumed from the inside. The way the room spun even when I closed my eyes.

And I remember calling for her.

"Mother—"

She comes. I can hear her footsteps. Measured. Slow.

She stands in the doorway, and for a moment—just a moment—I think I see something soften in her face. A flicker of concern. Of recognition that I am hers, and she is supposed to protect me.

But then her expression closes.

Like a door.

She turns to one of the younger priestesses, a girl barely older than me. "Tend to the others first," she says. "If the gods will her to survive, she will."

And she leaves.

Not forever. Just...away. To the other rooms. To the children of other women. To people she deems more worthy of saving.

I am twelve years old, burning with fever, and my mother has decided I am not a priority.

I survive—barely.

But something in me doesn't.

The part that believed love could be earned—that if I was just good enough, obedient enough, useful enough—dies in that room.

And in its place, something colder grows.

Resentment. Rage. The kind that doesn't scream. The kind that calculates.

I learn to watch her the way she watches the temple's enemies—carefully, strategically, looking for weaknesses.

I learn that proximity to someone does not equal safety.

I learn that a mother's love is not guaranteed, even when blood says it should be.

And I learn that betrayal doesn't always come with a knife.

Sometimes it comes with absence.

Sometimes it's just a woman walking away while you burn.

I died young in that life. Sixteen, maybe seventeen.

Not from the fever. From something quieter. A wasting sickness the healers couldn't name or heal. The kind that happens when a soul decides the body isn't worth fighting for anymore.

My mother performed the burial rites.

She said the prayers with perfect precision, her voice unwavering.

And as they laid me in the ground, wrapped in linen, surrounded by oils and amulets meant to guide me into the afterlife—

I felt nothing from her.

No grief. No regret. No love finally freed by death.

Just duty.

I was a task completed. A daughter dispatched. An inconvenience resolved.

And as my soul lifted from that body, hovering for a moment before the gravity of the next realm pulled me forward—

I made a vow.

Not consciously. Not with words.

But the energy was clear, sharp, undeniable—

I will follow this wound until I understand it.

And when I find the truth—it ends with me.

I gasped.

"What do you see now?"

I couldn't speak yet. My throat was too tight. My chest—

The heaviness was worse. Like it had doubled.

Pam watched me carefully. "Tell me."

I told her. Egypt. The temple. The fever. My mother walking

away.

She listened without interrupting, nodding occasionally.

When I finished, she was quiet for a moment.

"How does your body feel right now?" she asked.

"Heavy," I said, pressing my hand to my chest again. "Like, I can't breathe all the way."

"That's the grief," she said. "The rejection. It's stored in your heart space. You've been carrying it—not just from this lifetime, but from that one too."

"We need to do some clearing work. I want do a scan first, and then we'll do some healing on your heart space. Okay?"

I nodded.

The Clearing

Pam had me close my eyes again and guided me through a body scan.

"I'm going to check your energy field, each chakra, to see if there's anything attached to you that doesn't belong. Just breathe and let me know if you feel anything unusual."

She worked quietly, methodically. "Now, let's work on the heart."

After a few minutes, she spoke.

"You're clear," she said. "No attachments. No cords. Whatever this energy is—whatever's happening in your maternal line—it's not on you. You're protected."

I felt a wave of relief. "So, I'm...okay?"

"You're safe," she confirmed. "But that doesn't mean you're not carrying pain. You are. It's just your pain—the emotional residue from lifetimes of rejection. It's stored in your body, especially your heart space. And we're going to work on releasing some of that right now."

Heart Space Healing

She guided me back into a light trance.

"I want you to focus on your heart," she said. "Imagine it as a room. What does it look like?"

I closed my eyes and saw it immediately: a small room, dim, cluttered. Heavy curtains blocking the light. And in the center, a weight—dark, dense, like a dark stone.

"I see a stone," I said. "It's heavy. It's sitting right in the middle."

"Very good," Pam said. "That's the grief. The rejection. The pain you've been carrying. I want you to pick it up. Feel its weight. And then I want you to ask it: What do you need me to know?"

I imagined myself lifting the stone. It was heavier than I expected.

And then, quietly, I heard the answer—not in words, but in feeling:

I have been waiting to be seen.

Tears came, hot and fast.

"It's okay," Pam said softly. "Let it come. This is the release."

She guided me through the process—acknowledging the pain, thanking it for protecting me, and then gently, intentionally, setting it down outside the room.

"You don't have to carry this anymore," she said. "It's not yours to hold. You can leave it here, in this session, and walk away lighter."

I imagined setting the stone down. And as I did, the room in my heart shifted—curtains pulled back, light streaming in, space opening up.

When I opened my eyes, I felt different.

Not healed completely. But lighter.

I came out of the trance and sat up on the couch.

Pam's office drifted back into focus—the sandalwood, the soft lighting, the present moment I'd temporarily vacated.

My face was wet. I was crying, though I didn't remember starting.

"Take your time," Pam said softly, handing me tissues. "Very good. Breathe. You're safe. You're here."

The Wrap Up

Pam handed me water and gave me a moment to ground.

"How do you feel?" she asked.

"Lighter," I said. "But also…confused. I don't understand why she keeps showing up in my life—not to love me—to harm me. Why does it keep happening? Why does she always—" I stopped, unable to finish.

"That's what we're going to figure out," Pam said calmly. "This work isn't just about seeing the past—it's about understanding the patterns so you can break them."

She paused, choosing her words carefully.

"What you experienced today—the coldness, the abandonment, the rejection—that's real. That's your trauma. You're seeing your mother in dreams. I feel this is deeply-rooted—ancestral and not isolated to you. We're going to continue processing it. But I also want you to consider something."

I waited.

"You said your grandmother raised you. And she loved you?"

"Yes, completely."

"So it didn't touch her. Whatever this is—whatever runs in your maternal line—it looks like it skipped her or she broke free of it."

I hadn't thought of it that way.

"That tells me," Pam continued, "that this isn't just about you and your mother. This is generational. There's something in the bloodline. And your mother is likely carrying it."

"But not me?"

"Not you," she confirmed. "You're clear. But that doesn't mean you're not affected by it. You've been on the receiving end of it your whole life—this life and others. And that's what we're healing."

She leaned forward.

"Listen to me carefully. You can't heal her. Whatever she carries is hers to face. The only work assigned to you is your own healing. Process your pain. Do your work. Break the cycle so it doesn't continue with you."

I sat with that for a moment.

"So...what do I do?"

"You keep doing this work," Pam said. "We'll access more lifetimes if you're ready. We'll continue clearing the pain from your heart space. And along the way, we'll piece the puzzle together so you can see it clearly and make a choice about what you want to do with it."

She handed me a card with her contact information.

"I want to see you again in two weeks for an integration session. Between now and then, drink plenty of water. Ground. Journal anything that comes up—dreams, emotions, body sensations. Don't push them away. Let them surface so we can work with them."

"And if it gets overwhelming?"

"Call me. Don't sit with it alone."

I left her office feeling different—raw, but also strangely hopeful.

I wasn't broken.

I wasn't carrying some entity or curse.

I was just carrying pain.

And this kind of pain, I was learning, could be released.

But as I sat there in Pam's parking lot, one question kept circling in my mind:

If this thing isn't on me—if it's on her—then what is it? And how far back does it go?

I didn't have the answer yet.

But I knew I was going to find it.

CHAPTER 3
What Survived the Fire

I didn't go straight home.

I sat in my car in Pam's parking lot for twenty minutes, hands resting on the steering wheel, staring out the window.

The session had ended. She'd cleared me, healed my heart space, given me water, instructions, and her card for emergencies.

But my body hadn't fully returned to the present yet.

I could still feel the sand. The heat. The way my twelve-year-old lungs had struggled to pull in air while fever burned through me like wildfire.

I could still see her face—not the face she wears now, but the one she wore then. Different features. Same eyes. Same expression when she looked at me.

Adequate.

The word had followed me across lifetimes.

I finally turned the key. Started the engine. Drove home on autopilot, my hands remembering the route even though my mind was still three thousand years away.

My apartment felt too bright when I walked in. Too modern. Too now.

I dropped my keys on the black marble counter and stood in the kitchen, unsure what to do with my body. Eat? Shower? Pretend this was a normal Tuesday afternoon?

Instead, I walked to my altar.

It was small—a corner table draped in deep purple cloth, covered in the tools I'd collected over years of seeking. Candles. Crystals. A wild turkey feather I found in the front yard of my old house. My grandmother's cowrie shells, still in the leather pouch she'd kept them in, worn soft from decades of handling.

And my tarot deck.

I hadn't planned to do a reading. Pam had said to rest. Ground. Be gentle with myself.

But my hands were already reaching for the cards.

Because I needed to know.

Was Egypt the only one?

Or was it worse than I thought?

I lit a candle. White. For clarity.

I called on my Ancestors to help me find the truth. To protect me.

Took three deep breaths, the way Pam had taught me. Centered myself as much as I could, which wasn't much.

Shuffled the cards, asking the questions silently:

What do I need to see? Show me the scope. How many lifetimes has she been my enemy?

I pulled one card.

The Tower.

Of course.

I almost laughed—almost.

I pulled another.

Eight of Swords. A woman bound, blindfolded, surrounded by blades.

Trapped. Unable to see. Imprisoned by circumstances she can't escape.

Another card.

Five of Cups. Spilled cups. Grief. Loss. Looking at what's been destroyed instead of what remains.

Another.

Ten of Swords. A body face-down, ten blades in the back. Betrayal. The worst has already happened.

My hand trembled as I laid the cards out in a line.

I kept pulling.

Three of Swords. A heart pierced. Sorrow that cuts to the bone.

Nine of Swords. Nightmares. Anxiety. The terror that wakes you at 3 a.m.

Seven of Swords. Deception. Theft. Someone taking what isn't theirs.

I stopped when I'd laid out twelve cards.

Every single one was a card of pain.

Not one card of hope. Not one reversal. Not one glimmer of relief.

I sat back, staring at the spread.

"Okay," I whispered to the empty room. To the universe. To Spirit. To whatever was listening. "I hear you."

I knew I needed more than tarot.

I needed confirmation. Details. Specificity.

I reached for my grandmother's cowrie shells.

She'd taught me how to read them when I was in my late

twenties, before she died. Sitting at her kitchen table, her wrinkled hands guiding mine, showing me how to cast them, how to interpret the patterns they made when they fell.

"These don't lie," she'd said. "People lie. Even cards can be read wrong if your mind's too loud. But the shells? They tell the truth whether you're ready or not."

I poured them into my palm. Six shells, smooth and small, each one carrying decades of her questions, her prayers, her divination.

I held them against my chest for a moment.

Grandma, if you're listening—I need you to help me see this clearly.

I cast them onto the cloth.

They landed in a formation I recognized immediately.

Chaos. Conflict. Repetition.

I asked the question aloud this time, my voice steadier than I felt:

"How many lifetimes has my mother been my enemy?"

I cast again.

The shells fell.

I counted the pattern, read the positions, cross-referenced what my grandmother had taught me.

The answer came through clearly, cold as ice—

All of them.

Every life where your souls have intersected, she has been the one who harms you.

Not sometimes. Not accidentally.

Enemy. Not adversary. Adversaries meet on even ground. This was not that.

An enemy is placed.

This one wore my mother's face.

Every. Single. Time.

I thought I'd cry.

I thought the weight of it—the confirmation that this wasn't one bad life, one unfortunate incarnation, but a force stretching back through centuries—would break me.

Instead, I felt something else.

Clarity.

Cold, sharp, undeniable clarity.

This wasn't my fault.

I hadn't failed to earn her love in this lifetime. There was no version of me—no more obedient child, no quieter daughter, no better performance—that would have changed the outcome.

Because it wasn't me.

It had never been about me.

This was something older. Deeper. Something running through the bloodline, and I had been living on the receiving end of it without knowing the full extent.

But now I knew.

And knowing changed everything.

I stayed up until 9 p.m., sitting at my altar, pulling cards, casting shells, taking notes in a journal that was filling up too fast.

I made a list of the lifetimes I could sense but hadn't fully accessed yet:

Egypt, ancient. (She didn't try to help me).

New Orleans. Late 1800s, maybe early 1900s? (A house with red curtains. The daughter of a madam. Shame that lived in my bones. Her face painted, beautiful, cold.)

South Carolina. 1900s. (My mother chose a white man over me).

Others I can't see clearly yet—shadows, fragments, flashes of faces I almost recognize.

The pattern was undeniable.

Different centuries. Different circumstances. Different roles.

But always the same energy.

Always her.

Always the betrayal.

I set my pen down and stared at the list.

A thought occurred to me then, sharp and uncomfortable:

What if I'm not the only one stuck in this loop?

What if she's trapped in it too?

Not as the victim—she'd made that abundantly clear. But what if whatever had started this, whatever original wound or pattern had locked us together—what if she didn't know how to break it either?

What if she was just as bound to this as I was, repeating it because it was the only script she knew?

Or worse—

What if something was using her?

I thought about what Pam had said:

"Your grandmother loved you. The pattern didn't touch her. That tells me it skipped her—or she broke free of it."

My grandmother had been my mother's mother. Same bloodline. Same family.

But she had loved me.

Fiercely. Completely. Without condition.

She had recognized me in a way my mother never had. Like she'd known me before. Like our souls had found each other and said, Oh. There you are.

If the wound ran in the bloodline, why had it skipped her?

Or, had it not skipped her—had she just been strong enough to fight it off?

I opened my journal to a fresh page and wrote at the top:

WHAT IF IT'S NOT JUST HER?

Underneath, I started listing possibilities:

- A pattern. A generational curse. Something passed down that she inherited.

- Something attached to her. Not to me—Pam said I was clear. But to her.

- A spiritual wound so old it predates both of us. Something that happened generations ago and never healed, just kept repeating.

- An earthbound soul? Someone who didn't cross over and latched onto the maternal line?

I stopped writing and stared at the list.

None of these options absolved her.

Even if something was moving through her, using her, influencing her—she still made choices. She still caused harm. She still looked at me, lifetime after lifetime, and chose cruelty.

But it would explain why the energy felt so consistent.

Why it didn't feel like a person making different choices in different contexts.

It felt like something repetitive. Mechanical. Like a program running in the background, executing the same commands over and over.

I pulled one more card before I went to bed.

Not asking about me this time.

Asking about her.

Show me what's moving through my mother. Show me what I'm really dealing with.

I closed my eyes, shuffled, pulled.

The card I turned over made my breath catch.

The Moon.

Illusion. Secrets. Things hidden in darkness. Ancestral trauma. The subconscious mind. Deception—but also self-deception. A woman who doesn't even know she's lost.

I turned the deck over. Underneath it, on the bottom, one card lay anchored for me to see.

I picked it up.

The Devil.

Chains. Bondage. Patterns you can't escape—or think you can't. Being trapped in a cycle and believing you have no choice.

I set both cards on the altar and stared at them.

"You're stuck too," I whispered. "Aren't you?"

The candle flickered.

I didn't know if that was a yes or just the air conditioning kicking on.

But I felt something shift in the room.

In me.

I didn't forgive her.

I wasn't anywhere close to that.

But I understood, in that moment, that whatever I was about to uncover—it wasn't going to be simple.

It was going to be layers. Generations. A wound that went deeper than either of us.

And if I wanted to break the cycle, I couldn't just focus on the harm done to me.

I was going to have to understand the whole picture.

Not to excuse her.

But to see clearly enough to finally cut myself free.

I crawled into bed at 9 p.m., exhausted but wired.

I set an intention before I fell asleep:

Show me the next life. The next betrayal. Help me understand the cycle so I can break it.

I didn't expect an answer right away.

But when I finally slept, the dreams came fast and vivid.

And this time, I wasn't in Egypt.

I was somewhere that smelled like magnolias and old wood.

Somewhere humid and close.

Somewhere that felt like secrets kept behind red velvet curtains.

New Orleans.

And I could already feel her presence.

Waiting.

CHAPTER 4
Integration Is Not Peace

Two weeks passed before I saw Pam again.

She'd told me to journal, to ground, to be gentle with myself.

I tried.

But gentle wasn't what came.

The first week after Egypt, I barely slept.

Every time I closed my eyes, I was back in that room—stone walls, fever burning through me, calling for a mother who wouldn't come. I'd wake up gasping, my chest tight, the heaviness Pam had cleared trying to creep back in.

So I stayed awake.

I worked. Saw clients. Did consultations for other people—helped them untangle their problems, their shadows, their wounds—while carefully managing my own.

But at night, I went to my altar.

I pulled cards obsessively. Cast the shells until my hands ached. Asked the same questions over and over, hoping for a different answer.

How many lifetimes?

All of them.

Why?

The cards wouldn't say. Or couldn't. Or maybe I wasn't asking the right question yet.

By the second week, something shifted.

The dreams changed.

I wasn't in Egypt anymore.

Now I smelled magnolias. Heard piano music drifting through humid air. Felt red velvet under my fingers and shame settling into my bones like it had always lived there.

New Orleans, I thought. That's next.

I showed up to Pam's office on a Thursday afternoon, carrying a journal filled with two weeks' worth of notes, dreams, and divination readings.

She took one look at me and smiled warmly.

"You didn't rest, did you?"

"I tried," I said, sitting down. "But there's too much coming up. I couldn't stop."

"Show me," she said, gesturing to the journal.

I opened it and walked her through everything: the tarot spreads that showed only pain, the cowrie shells confirming a consistent thread spanned all lifetimes, the dreams shifting from Egypt to somewhere else.

She listened without interrupting, occasionally nodding, her face calm but focused.

When I finished, she sat back in her chair.

"You've been doing the work," she said. "That's good. But I also want to make sure you're not drowning in it. How's your body feeling?"

I pressed my hand to my chest. "Heavy again. Not as bad as before, but…it's there."

"That's normal," she said. "Heart space healing isn't one-and-done. Grief has layers. We'll work on it again today before we go any deeper."

She paused, studying me.

"But first, I want to talk about what you found. You said the shells told you this energy spans all lifetimes—every time you and your mother's energy have intersected, she's been the one who harms you."

"Yes."

"And you also said your grandmother loved you completely. Hmmm…and the energy didn't touch her."

I nodded.

Pam leaned forward, choosing her words carefully.

"Here's what I'm seeing. This isn't just about you and your mother having a difficult relationship across a few lifetimes. This is ancestral. This is a *pattern* that runs through the maternal line—but selectively. It didn't attach to your grandmother. It skipped her, or she was strong enough to reject it. But your mother…"

She trailed off, watching my face.

"She's carrying it," I finished.

"Yes," Pam said. "And as I said before: It's not your place to heal her. You may love her. Wish differently for her. You may even understand her. But understanding does not require you to bleed for her. Her healing—her responsibility. She would have to choose to address it. And from what you've told me, she's not interested in doing that."

"She's not," I said quietly. "She doesn't even think there's a problem. She thinks I'm the problem."

Pam nodded, no surprise in her expression.

"That's how these energies work. The person carrying it often can't see it. They think everyone else is the issue. They're so identified with the wound, they don't even know where they end and it begins."

She let that sit for a moment.

"So the work we're doing here—it's not to fix her. It's to heal you. To help you see the pattern clearly enough that you can break it for yourself. So it doesn't continue with you. So you don't pass it to the next generation."

I felt something loosen in my chest.

"I'm not trying to save her," I said, testing the words.

"No," Pam confirmed. "You're trying to save yourself. And that's enough. That's everything."

We sat in silence for a moment—neither of us moved.

Then I asked the question that had been sitting in my throat for two weeks:

"Do you think it's an attachment? Like…an entity or an earthbound soul who didn't cross over or something…or is she just low-key diabolical?"

Pam didn't dismiss it.

"It's possible," she said, her voice measured. "But what catches my attention is the pattern. The energy appears the same way in every lifetime you've visited so far—different eras, different circumstances, yet the presence feels identical. When something repeats like that, it usually means there’s a deeper thread moving through the maternal line...something very old that hasn’t finished telling its story."

"But it skipped my grandmother."

"Yes. She was skipped," Pam confirmed. "Which tells me she either didn't match the frequency, or she had protection, or she consciously rejected it. Some people are just stronger that way. They refuse to be carriers."

I thought about my grandmother—her strength, her clarity, the way she'd loved me without hesitation.

"So what do I do?" I asked.

"We keep going," Pam said. "We access more lifetimes. We look for the pattern—not just the harm, but how it shows up. How it operates. What it feeds on. And eventually, if you're ready, we can look for the source. The original wound. The moment this attachment—or pattern, or curse, whatever it is—first latched onto your maternal line."

"And then what?"

"Then you decide," she said. "You can walk away. Cut the cord. Stay free of it and live your life. Or you can go deeper—try to understand the root, and heal your bloodline.

She smiled.

"Right now, let's just focus on the next step. You said you've been dreaming about New Orleans?"

"Yes. A house. Red curtains. Shame. And her—my mother's energy. I can feel her there."

Pam nodded. "That's the next lifetime calling you. Are you ready to access it?"

I thought about it.

Egypt had broken me open. Shown me the first betrayal.

But I needed to see more. Needed to understand the full scope before I could figure out how to break free.

"Yes," I said. "I'm ready."

Heart Space Check-In

Before we finished, Pam had me close my eyes.

"Let's check your heart space again. Same as last time—imagine it as a room. What does it look like now?"

I focused inward.

The room was lighter than before. The heavy weight I'd been carrying was gone—or at least, it wasn't sitting in the center anymore.

But there was still clutter. Shadows in the corners. A faint ache, like a bruise that hadn't fully healed.

"It's better," I said. "But there's still…something."

"That's okay," Pam said. "We're going to work on it. Healing happens in layers. Let's do a little clearing before you leave today."

She guided me through another release—this time focusing on the grief I'd been holding in my chest since childhood. The longing for a mother who never came. The belief that I wasn't enough.

By the time we finished, the space in my heart felt clearer. Lighter.

Not perfect. But breathable.

"Good," Pam said softly. "How does that feel?"

"Better," I said, opening my eyes. "Lighter."

She smiled. "That's the goal. Not perfection—just progress."

Closing

Pam handed me a bottle of water and let me sit for a moment, grounding back into the present.

"You've done really good work today," she said. "Processing Egypt, integrating what came up, clearing more from your heart space. That's a lot."

"It feels like a lot," I admitted.

"It is. Which is why I don't want to rush into another regression right now. You need time to sit with this. To let it settle. To see what else surfaces."

I nodded, relieved. Part of me had been bracing for her to say, *Let's go deeper today,* but I was exhausted. Emotionally drained.

"You said you've been dreaming about New Orleans?" Pam asked.

"Yes. Red curtains. A house. Her energy. It's been calling me."

"Then that's the next lifetime we'll access," Pam said. "But not today. I want you to take some time—at least a few weeks, maybe longer—to process what we've done so far. Take a hot sea salt bath with lavender and rosemary to cleanse your energy. Keep journaling. Keep doing your divination work and give yourself permission to just be. To rest."

She looked at me seriously.

"This work is deep. It's not a sprint. If you go too fast, you'll burn out. And we need you strong for what's coming."

"What's coming?" I asked.

"The source," she said simply. "Eventually, if you want to fully break this cycle, we're going to have to find where it started. The original entry point. But you're not ready for that yet. You need to see more of the pattern first. Understand it fully. So we'll do New Orleans next. And then we'll see where that leads."

She pulled out her calendar.

"Let's schedule you for another session. How does eight weeks sound? That gives you time to integrate, to dream, to let the next lifetime come into focus."

"Eight weeks," I repeated. It felt both too long and exactly right.

"You can always call me if something urgent comes up," Pam said. "But I think you'll benefit from the space. Let this settle. Trust the process."

I nodded and we scheduled the appointment.

As I gathered my things to leave, Pam said one more thing:

"Remember—you're not trying to save her—you can't. You're trying to free yourself. Don't lose sight of that."

"I won't," I said.

But as I walked out of her office and into the afternoon light, I wasn't sure if I believed it yet.

Because part of me still loves her. Part of me wanted to understand why.

Why she kept doing this.

Why the pattern was so relentless.

Why my grandmother had escaped it, but my mother couldn't.

And I had a feeling that New Orleans—whenever I finally got there—would show me something I wasn't prepared to see.

CHAPTER 5
The Pattern Strikes Back

The dreams started three days after the integration session.

Not subtle ones. Not the kind you half-remember in the morning and forget by noon.

These were the kind that pulled me under and held me there—vivid, suffocating, impossible to shake.

Week One

The first dream came on a Sunday night.

I was standing in front of a house I'd never seen but somehow knew. Three stories, wrought iron balconies, tall windows with heavy curtains the color of wine. The air was thick, humid, sweet with the smell of jasmine and something underneath it—rot, maybe, or just the scent of a city built on swampland.

I could hear music. Piano, slow and melancholic, drifting from somewhere inside.

And I knew, without seeing her, that she was in there.

Waiting.

I woke up at 3:30 a.m., heart pounding, the smell of magnolias still clinging to me like perfume I couldn't wash off.

I tried to go back to sleep.

Couldn't.

So I went to my altar and pulled a card.

What is New Orleans trying to show me?

The card I pulled was the **Five of Pentacles.**

Exclusion. Being left out in the cold. Poverty—not just material, but emotional. Spiritual. The sense of being abandoned while others live in warmth and plenty.

I stared at the card for a long time.

Then I wrote in my journal: She's going to leave me outside again. In some way. I can feel it.

Week Two

The dreams came every night now.

Sometimes I was a child in that house, watching women move

through rooms in silk and lace, their laughter sharp and practiced.

Sometimes I was older—fourteen, fifteen—standing in a doorway while men looked at me the way you look at something you're considering buying.

And always, always, she was there.

Beautiful. Untouchable. Cold.

My mother.

Though in the dream, she wasn't called that. She was Madame. Madame Colette.

And I was hers.

Not in the way a daughter belongs to a mother.

In the way property belongs to an owner.

I tried to function normally.

I worked. Saw clients. Made small talk with friends who asked how I was doing and accepted "fine" as an answer even though I looked like I hadn't slept in days.

Because I hadn't.

Every night, New Orleans.

Every morning, I woke up exhausted, my chest heavy, my throat tight with something I couldn't name yet.

Shame, maybe.

Or grief that had calcified into something harder.

Week Three - The Letter

It came on a Wednesday.

Not in the mail—email. Document attached. Five pages, single-spaced, my name at the top like she was writing a formal letter.

I saw her name in my inbox and my stomach dropped.

I hadn't heard from her in over a year. Maybe longer.

I stared at the email for ten minutes before I opened it.

I should have deleted it.

But part of me—that part that still loved her, that still hoped—needed to know what she wanted.

The letter started soft.

"Daughter. I've been thinking about you lately. Wondering how you are. I know we haven't spoken in a while, and I wanted to reach out…"

Sweet.

Almost maternal.

For half a page, I let myself believe it.

Then the shift came.

"I don't understand why you've shut me out of your life. I'm your mother. I carried you. I gave you life. And this is how you repay me? With silence? With coldness?"

The words got sharper.

"You've always been this way. Even as a child—so distant, so ungrateful. Stubborn. You never come to see me. Your grandmother spoiled you, turned you against me. I tried, but you never gave me a chance. You never appreciated anything I did."

I stopped reading for a moment, hands shaking, holding back the cuss words forming in my throat.

She never did anything.

She wasn't there.

She left.

But in her version of the story, I was the one who abandoned her. I'm the villain.

I kept reading.

"I've made mistakes, yes. But so have you. You act like you're so perfect, so innocent, so spiritual, but you've hurt me too. You don't know what it's been like for me. You don't know what I've been through."

Five pages of this BS.

Blame. Guilt. Projection.

By the end, I felt like I couldn't breathe.

She closed with:

"I hope one day you'll find it in your heart to forgive me for whatever you think I did. I'm not getting any younger you know. Life is short. I don't want to die with this distance between us. You need to change your ways before it's too late. But if my eyes close before yours—don't bother coming to my funeral. It will be too late."

I read that last part three times.

"Don't bother coming to my funeral. It will be too late."

"What?"

For a split second, I saw myself in an orange jumpsuit.

Not, *I'm sorry.*

Not, *I understand why you're hurt.*

Not even a genuine plea for reconciliation.

Just: I don't want to feel uncomfortable, so you need to change. You need to fix this. And if you don't, I'll punish you—even from the grave.

I closed my laptop.

My chest was burning.

I sat on the edge of my couch, lost in a liminal space, staring at nothing.

All the work I'd done with Pam—the clearing, the heart space healing, the understanding that I wasn't responsible for her—felt like it had been undone in five pages.

I felt heavy again.

Hollow.

Like I was twelve years old, standing in a doorway, watching her leave.

I tried to journal.

Tried to process it rationally.

But all I could write was:

Why does she keep doing this?

Does she have dementia? Is she crazy?

Why can't she just leave me alone?

Why does she think she has the right to reach into my life whenever she wants and rip me open again?

I called my best friend, Li.

Told her about the five-page email.

"Did you respond?" she asked.

"No."

"Good. Don't."

"But what if—"

"No," Li said firmly. "There's no 'what if.' She does this. She always does this. She waits until you've got some peace, and then she comes back to disturb it. You know this."

I did know this.

But knowing didn't make it hurt less.

"She said she doesn't want to die with distance between us," I said quietly.

Li was silent for a moment.

Then, "That's manipulation. She's trying to guilt you into breaking your boundaries. She's not sorry. She's not trying to repair anything. She just wants you to respond so she knows she still has access."

I closed my eyes.

"You're right."

"I know I am," Li said gently. "Delete the email. Don't respond. And call your therapist if you need to. But don't let her back in."

I didn't delete the email.

I moved it to a folder and closed my laptop.

Then I went to my altar and did a full divination spread.

What is this email really about? What is she trying to do?

The cards were clear:

Seven of Swords. Deception. Someone trying to take what isn't theirs.

The Devil. Manipulation. Chains. Someone trying to bind you to them.

Five of Cups. She's grieving the loss of control over me.

I sat back, staring at the spread.

She wasn't reaching out because she missed me.

She was reaching out because she'd lost control.

And she wanted it back.

I cast the cowrie shells.

Is this the pattern? Is this what she does in every lifetime?

The shells fell.

The answer…Yes.

She reaches for you. She manipulates. She binds. And when you try to break free, she punishes you.

I wrote in my journal:

Egypt: She walked away while I burned.

New Orleans: (I don't know the full story yet, but I can feel it—she won't let me leave.)

This life: She abandons me, then reaches back when it suits her. Tries to make me feel guilty for protecting myself.

Same pattern. Different methods.

I closed the journal and sat in my thoughts.

And I made a decision.

I wasn't going to respond.

Not now. Not ever.

She didn't get to have access to me or my energy anymore.

Week Four - The Text

Five days after the email, my phone buzzed.

A text—from her.

I stared at the notification, my heart racing.

I opened it.

"Hey! How's the weather over there? Did you get any snow? 😊 "

WTF?

No mention of the five-page letter.

No acknowledgment of the trauma dump, the blame, the guilt.

Just: How's the weather, snow, and a smiley face?

Like nothing had happened.

Like she hadn't just ripped me apart line by line last week.

I sat on my couch, staring at the text, and something in me snapped.

Not sadness—

Rage.

Cold, clear, undeniable rage.

She'd done it again.

The push-pull. The bait and switch.

Send a letter designed to wound, then follow it up with casual cheerfulness to make me look crazy if I reacted.

If I responded with anger, she'd say, "I was just asking about the weather. Why are you so sensitive? You're too dramatic."

If I ignored her, she'd tell people I was cold, ungrateful, cruel.

Either way, I lost.

That was the game.

That had always been the game.

I didn't respond to the text either.

Instead, I blocked her number.

I should have done it years ago.

But part of me had always kept that door cracked open just in case. Just in case she changed. Just in case she finally became the mother I needed.

But she wasn't going to change.

She was never going to change.

And I was done waiting.

I journaled that night:

She doesn't see me as a person. She sees me as a thing she's entitled to access. A toy she can pick up and put down whenever she wants.

And when I set boundaries, she doesn't respect them. She just finds new ways to cross them.

This is the pattern.

This is what she does.

And I'm breaking it.

"I'm done!"

Week Five

The dreams intensified after I blocked her.

Now I wasn't just seeing New Orleans.

I was living it.

I knew the layout of the house—which rooms were for tricks, which were private, where the kitchen was, where the back stairs led. I knew the names of the other women: Rosalie, Josephine, Marguerite. I knew the smell of the perfume my mother wore, the sound of her heels on hardwood, the way her voice changed depending on who she was talking to.

I knew I was fourteen.

And I knew what was coming.

I woke up every morning with my hands clenched into fists, my jaw aching from grinding my teeth all night.

My body remembered what my mind was still trying to deny.

Week Six

I called Pam.

"The dreams won't stop," I told her. "And my mother—she sent me an email. Five pages. Then texted me five days later like nothing happened."

"Did you respond?"

"No. I blocked her."

"Good," Pam said. There was no judgment in her voice. Just

calm support. "How do you feel about that decision?"

"Angry," I said. "And relieved. And guilty. All at the same time."

"That's normal," Pam said. "You're allowed to feel all of it. But I want you to notice something. She reached out right when you started accessing New Orleans. Right when you started getting close to understanding the pattern."

I hadn't thought about that.

"You think that's connected?"

"I think," Pam said carefully, "that on some level—energetically, spiritually, however you want to frame it—she sensed you were pulling away. Really pulling away. And she tried to pull you back."

I sat with that.

"The email, the text—that's the same pattern you're seeing in the past lives. Control. Manipulation. Refusing to let you leave."

"Yeah," I said quietly. "It is."

"And you blocked her," Pam said. "You set the boundary. You chose yourself. That's huge."

I didn't feel huge.

I felt exhausted.

"The New Orleans dreams are intense," I said. "I don't think I can wait the full eight weeks. I need to do the session."

"Okay," Pam said. "I have an opening this Friday. Virtual session okay? You can do it from home, in your own space. Might actually be easier for this one."

I agreed immediately.

Virtual felt safer somehow. Like I could access the lifetime but still have my own sacred space around me. My altar. My grandmother's shells. The things that were familiar and reminded me I wasn't trapped there anymore.

We scheduled for Friday at 2 p.m.

The Night Before the Session

I prepared my space.

Cleaned my altar. Lit white candles for protection and clarity. Burned sage and palo santo until my apartment smelled like a botanica.

I pulled one last card.

What do I need to know before I go into New Orleans?

The card that flew out was the **Eight of Swords.**

A woman bound and blindfolded, surrounded by swords, trapped—but the bindings are loose. She could free herself if she realized the cage was an illusion.

I studied the card for a long time.

Then I wrote in my journal:

Whatever I see tomorrow—however bad it is—I need to remember: I'm not trapped there anymore. That life is over. I survived it. And I'm going back to witness it, to understand it, to finally let it go.

Just like I'm not trapped with her in this life either. I blocked her. I set the boundary. I chose myself.

I'm not that girl anymore—not in New Orleans, not in this life.

I'm the woman who's breaking the cycle.

I set the card on my altar and went to bed.

For the first time in weeks, I didn't dream.

Friday Morning

The next morning, I woke up calm.

Ready.

At 1:58 p.m., I logged into Zoom.

The Zoom window opened at exactly 2 p.m.

CHAPTER 6
Where Blood Learned to Bargain (New Orleans)

Pam's face appeared on my screen—calm, grounded, present. Her office behind her looked the same as it had in person: warm lighting, books on shelves, a sense of safety embedded in the space.

"Hi," she said, smiling. "How are you feeling?"

"Nervous," I admitted. "But ready."

"Good. Nervous means you're taking this seriously. That's healthy." She leaned forward slightly. "I want you to look around your space. What do you see?"

I looked around my room. My altar was visible to the left—candles lit, my grandmother's cowrie shells in their pouch, crystals arranged carefully. White sage smoke was still lingering in the air from the clearing I'd done last night.

"That's perfect," Pam said. "You've created sacred space. That's going to support you through this session. You're not just accessing a past life—you're doing it surrounded by protection, by your ancestors, by your own power."

I nodded, feeling slightly steadier.

"Before we go under," Pam continued, "I want to check in about the email and the text from your mother. How are you feeling about that now?"

"Angry," I said. "And clear. I blocked her. I'm not responding. I'm done."

"Good," Pam said, and I could hear the approval in her voice. "That was the right choice. And I want you to hold onto that clarity as we go into New Orleans. Because what you're about to see—it's going to echo what just happened. The control. The refusal to let you go. The punishment when you try to leave."

She paused.

"The difference is, in New Orleans, you didn't have the power to block her. You were trapped. But now? You're free. You've already recognized the pattern in this lifetime. What we're doing today is witnessing the past so you can fully break it and release it."

I took a deep breath.

"I'm ready."

Going Under

Pam's voice shifted—slower, softer, the hypnotic cadence I recognized from our first session.

"Close your eyes. Take a deep breath in…and let it out. Feel your body sinking into the chair. Feel the ground beneath you. You are safe. You are protected. You are held by your ancestors and your own power."

I let my eyes close.

My breathing slowed.

The sounds of my apartment—the hum of the refrigerator, the distant traffic outside—began to fade.

"I want you to go back," Pam said. "Back to the lifetime that's been calling you. The one with the red curtains. The one where your mother's energy is waiting. Let yourself move toward it. Don't force it. Just allow it to come into focus."

I felt the shift almost immediately.

The air changed—became heavier, warmer, humid.

I smelled magnolias.

And then I was there.

New Orleans, 1891

I am standing in a bedroom on the second floor of the house.

The room is beautiful in a way that feels designed—red velvet curtains, a four-poster bed with lace canopy, a vanity covered in perfume bottles and powder boxes. Gaslight flickers from the sconces on the walls, casting soft shadows.

I am fourteen years old.

My name, in this life—is Céleste.

And I am being dressed.

Hands—not mine, are fastening the buttons on a corset, pulling it tight until I can barely breathe. My hair is being pinned up, curled, arranged. Perfume is dabbed at my wrists, behind my ears, at the hollow of my throat.

I look at myself in the mirror.

I am beautiful.

And I am terrified.

"Tell me what you see," Pam's voice said, distant but steady, anchoring me.

"I'm in a bedroom," I said, my voice sounding strange to my own ears. "Getting dressed. Someone's helping me—one of the women who works here. Her name is…Josephine."

"Good. Stay with it. What's happening?"

"It's my first time," I said, and even as I said it, I felt nausea rise in my throat. "My mother—she's…she runs this house. And tonight, she's introducing me to a client."

I could feel the weight of it in my body—the shame, the inevitability, the trapped feeling of knowing what's coming and being powerless to stop it.

There's a knock at the door.

Josephine finishes pinning my hair and steps back, looking at me with something like pity in her eyes.

"You look perfect, chérie," she says softly. "Just remember—don't fight. It's easier if you don't fight."

The door opens.

My mother walks in.

She is quite beautiful in this life—caramel-colored skin, dark eyes that assess everything, a dress that fits her like it was painted on. Her hair is piled high, adorned with jewels. She moves like she owns not just this house, but the air itself.

Madame Colette.

She stops in front of me, studying me the way you'd study a piece of merchandise.

"Beautiful," she says, almost to herself. Then, to Josephine—"Leave us."

Josephine hesitates for a moment, then slips out of the room.

My mother circles me slowly.

"You'll do well tonight," she says. "Étienne is a generous man. He's paying well for the privilege of being your first. Don't disappoint me."

I want to speak. Want to beg her not to make me do this.

But the words won't come.

I already know: begging won't work.

It never works.

"How do you feel in this moment?" Pam's voice asked.

"Trapped," I said. My throat felt tight. "Like I can't breathe. Like I'm screaming inside but no sound is coming out."

"Stay with it. You're safe. You're just witnessing. What happens next?"

My mother touches my face to examine it—assessing it with no affection. She is making sure I will bring in the price she set.

"You're lucky," she says. "Not every girl gets this kind of opportunity. I'm giving you a future. A way to survive. You should be grateful."

I don't feel grateful.

I feel like I'm dying.

But I nod.

Because that's what she wants.

And when you're fourteen and your mother is the only person who stands between you and the street, you do what she wants.

She smiles—pleased.

"Good girl. Now come. Étienne is waiting downstairs."

She turns and walks toward the door, expecting me to follow.

I do.

Because I don't know what else to do.

The rest of the night is a blur of sensation I don't want to remember but can't forget.

A man's hands. The smell of cigar smoke and whiskey. Pain. Shame so deep it feels like it's embedded in my bones.

And through it all, I can hear music playing downstairs—piano, laughter, the sound of a party continuing as if nothing is happening.

As if I'm not being destroyed by a monster in a room upstairs.

When it's over, the man—Étienne, leaves money on the dresser.

Moments later, my mother comes back into the room.

She counts the bills, smiling.

"You did well," she says, like she's praising me for completing a chore. "Better than I expected for your first time."

She pockets the money.

Then she looks at me—still sitting on the bed, unable to move, my body feeling like it belongs to someone else.

"Go clean yourself up," she says. "You have another client in an hour."

And she leaves.

"Take a deep breath. You're doing so well," Pam's voice said reassuringly. "I know that was hard. Let's move forward. I want you to go to another significant moment in that lifetime. Something that shows the pattern clearly."

I felt the scene shift.

Time passed—days, weeks, maybe months.

And then I was standing in a different room.

I am sixteen now.

Two years have passed, though it feels like a lifetime.

I've learned how to perform. How to smile when I don't mean it. How to make men believe I want them when all I want is to disappear.

I've learned how to survive.

But I haven't learned how to escape.

There's a man who comes to the house regularly now.

His name is Christophe.

He doesn't come as a trick—he's a musician, plays piano in the parlor downstairs during parties.

And he sees me.

Not the version my mother has created—the trained, polished, expensive girl.

He sees me.

The part of me that's still a child. Still afraid. Still hoping for a way out.

We talk sometimes, when no one's watching. It was fun to steal a few minutes here and there. Nothing improper—just conversation. Connection.

And slowly, impossibly, I start to believe that maybe there's a life outside this house.

Maybe I don't have to stay here forever.

One night, after a party, Christophe pulls me aside.

"Come with me," he whispers. "I'm leaving New Orleans. Going west. You can come with me. We'll start over. You'll be free."

I stare at him, my heart pounding.

"She'll never let me go," I say.

"Then don't ask her permission," he says. "Just leave. Meet me tomorrow night. Midnight. The back gate. I'll be waiting."

I want to say yes.

Every part of me wants to say yes.

But I'm terrified.

Because I know my mother.

I know what she does to people who try to leave.

"What do you do?" Pam asked.

"I say yes," I whispered. "I pack a bag. I hide it under my bed. And I wait."

The next night, I slip out of my room just before midnight.

The house is quiet. My mother is in her private quarters, counting money, managing her empire.

I move down the back stairs, careful not to make a sound.

My heart is racing.

I can taste freedom.

I'm almost to the back door when I hear her voice.

"Going somewhere?"

I freeze.

Turn around.

My mother is standing at the top of the stairs, arms crossed, her face calm but her eyes cold.

"I—"

"Don't bother lying," she says. "I already know. Josephine told me."

My stomach drops.

Josephine. The woman who'd dressed me for my first night. Who'd looked at me with pity.

She told.

My mother descends the stairs slowly, each step deliberate.

"Did you really think you could leave me?" she asks, voice soft but sharp as a blade. "Did you think I wouldn't find out?"

"I just want to leave. I want to be free," I say, my voice breaking. "Please. I can't do this anymore."

She stops in front of me.

And for a moment—just a moment—I think I see something

shift in her face.

Recognition. Maybe even regret.

But then it's gone.

"You are free," she says. "Free to stay here, where you're fed and clothed and protected. Free to make a living doing work most girls would kill for. You think the world out there will be kinder to you than I am?"

She reaches out and grips my chin, forcing me to look at her.

"You will never leave me, Céleste. Do you know why?"

I don't answer.

"Because everything you are, I made. This face, this body, this life—it's mine. You belong to me. And no man, no dream, no fantasy of escape will ever change that."

She releases me.

"Now go back to your room. And pray I don't decide you need to be reminded of your place."

I don't go back to my room.

I go to the back gate.

Christophe isn't there.

I wait for an hour. Two.

He never comes.

I find out later—through whispers, through fragments of conversations I'm not supposed to hear—that my mother sent men to find him.

Some say she paid him off. Gave him enough money to leave the city and never come back.

Others say it was worse than that.

That he refused the money.

That he didn't leave willingly.

I never find out the truth.

But I know one thing for certain—

My mother made sure he was gone.

And she made sure I knew she was the one who did it.

"Move forward," Pam's voice said hypnotically. "To the end of that lifetime. Let's see how it ends."

I am twenty-one.

I've stopped trying to leave.

Stopped imagining a different life.

I've become exactly what my mother shaped and molded me to

be— beautiful, expensive, empty.

Men pay extraordinary amounts for me.

My mother collects every dollar.

And I go through the motions, day after day, my body present but my soul long gone.

I don't remember deciding to die.

But I remember the Laudanum.

The bottle in my hand.

The quiet certainty that this was the only way out.

If I couldn't leave through the door, I'd leave another way.

They found me in the morning.

Still and cold, dressed in the silk nightgown my mother had bought me because it *"presented well."*

My mother wept at my funeral.

Performed grief beautifully, the way she'd taught me to perform everything else.

But I was already gone by then—hovering somewhere above my body, watching.

I saw the truth in her face, even through the tears.

Relief.

I had been profitable.

But I had also been hers—a daughter, a reminder of something human she'd had to suppress to survive in the world she'd built.

My death freed her.

She could mourn the asset.

But she was glad the daughter was gone.

I came back to the present slowly, like surfacing from deep water.

When I opened my eyes, I was in my apartment.

Pam's face was on the screen, patient and steady.

"Welcome back," she said softly. "Take your time. Breathe."

I couldn't speak yet.

My face was wet with tears I didn't remember shedding.

My chest felt like someone had scraped it out.

"What did you see?" Pam asked.

I told her.

All of it.

The grooming. The first client. Christophe. The attempted escape. The way she made sure I could never leave.

My death.

When I finished, Pam was quiet for a moment.

"How does your body feel right now?"

"Heavy," I said. "Like I can't breathe. Like I'm still trapped there."

"You're not trapped," Pam said firmly. "You're here. You're safe. That life is over. You survived it. And now you're witnessing it so you can finally let it go."

She paused.

"Do you see the pattern?"

I nodded, even though the movement hurt.

"Egypt, she walked away while I burned. New Orleans, she kept me trapped, used me, and when I tried to leave, she made sure I couldn't. And in this life…"

I stopped, the realization hitting me like a wave.

"She's still doing it. The email. The text. The refusal to let me go. It's the same thing. Just a different method."

"Very good," Pam said. "That's exactly right."

Clearing and Grounding

"Before we end," Pam said, "we need to do some clearing. That was intense, and you're carrying a lot right now. Close your eyes."

I did.

She guided me through a body scan, checking for any residual energy from the session.

"Your heart space," she said. "There's tightness there. Shame. Let's work on releasing it."

She walked me through the same process as before—visualizing the room in my heart, seeing the weight I was carrying, acknowledging it, and then setting it down.

This time, the weight was different.

Not a stone.

A chain.

Wrapped around my heart, binding it, constricting it.

"I see a chain," I said.

"Good," Pam said. "That's the bondage. The feeling of being owned. I want you to grab that chain and remove it. You have the power to do that. It's not locked. You can take it off."

I imagined my hands gripping the chain.

It was heavier than I expected.

But I pulled.

And slowly, link by link, it loosened.

Fell away.

When it was gone, the room in my heart flooded with light.

I gasped.

"Good," Pam said. "You did it. How does that feel?"

"Lighter," I said. "Like I can breathe again."

Closing

Pam had me drink water. Ground. Look around my room and name five things I could see.

"You did incredible work today," she said. "That was one of the hardest lifetimes you're going to access. And you moved through it with so much strength."

"It doesn't feel like strength," I said.

"It is," Pam insisted. "You went into one of the most painful memories your soul carries, and you witnessed it without running. That's courage."

She paused.

"I want you to rest for the next few days. Journal if things come up, but don't push. Let this integrate. And we'll schedule another session in a few weeks to continue."

"There's more?" I asked, even though I already knew the answer.

"There's more," Pam confirmed. "But you don't have to do it all at once. We're peeling back layers. And each one you release, you get closer to freedom."

After we ended the call, I sat in my apartment soaking in the silence.

The candles on my altar had burned down to stubs.

The smell of sage had dissipated.

But I could still smell magnolias.

Still feel the weight of the corset around my ribs.

Still hear my mother's voice—

"You will never leave me."

But I had left her.

In that life, I'd left through death.

In this life, I'd left by blocking her number, by setting boundaries, by choosing myself.

And she hated it.

Because control was all she knew.

And I was finally, finally slipping free.

I pulled one card before bed.

What do I need to know after today?

The card that jumped out was the **Six of Swords**.

Transition. Moving away from turbulent waters toward calmer shores. The journey isn't over, but you're moving in the right direction.

I set the card on my altar and whispered to the empty room:

"I'm not yours anymore. Not in that life. Not in this one. I'm free."

And for the first time, I almost believed it.

CHAPTER 7
The Celebration

Three weeks had passed since the New Orleans session.

I was still processing.

Still journaling. Still doing clearing work. Still waking up some mornings with the scent of magnolias in my nose and shame sitting heavy on my chest.

Pam had told me to be gentle with myself. To rest. To let it integrate.

I was trying.

But the universe—or my mother, or whatever force refused to let me have peace—had other plans.

It was a Saturday morning.

I was sitting on my couch having a cup of coffee, half-watching something on TV, when my phone rang.

My cousin Jaenelle.

I smiled and answered. "Hey Jae, what's up?"

There was a pause on the other end. Not a good pause.

"Hey cuz," she said, and I could hear the hesitation in her voice. "I need to tell you something. And I'm only telling you because I think you should know. I don't want to upset you, but…yeah. You need to know."

My stomach dropped.

"What happened?"

Another pause.

"Your mom FaceTimed me yesterday."

Of course she did.

"She wants me to help her plan a surprise birthday party for Lisa."

Lisa. Jaenelle's older sister. My first cousin. My aunt's other daughter.

"Okay," I said slowly, already feeling the ground shifting under me.

"Yeah," Jaenelle continued. "She wants to go all out. Venue, catering, decorations, the whole thing. She's talking about inviting the whole family, making it this big celebration. And she asked me to help coordinate everything since it's supposed to be a *surprise*."

I didn't say anything.

Because I already knew where this was going.

"So, we're on FaceTime," Janelle said, "and she's going through the details—guest list, cake, decorations—and I'm sitting there thinking, Wait. Does she realize?"

"Realize what?" I asked, even though I knew.

"That you and Lisa have the same birthday," Jaenelle said. "You're only a year apart. Same day—every year."

My chest tightened.

"So, I told her," Jaenelle continued. "I said, 'Auntie, you know you're going to have to do *two* of everything, right? Two cakes. Two cards. Two sets of decorations. Everything doubled."

I held my breath. My chest began to tighten.

"And she looked at me through the screen—just stared at me—and said, 'Why would I need two of everything?"

There it was.

"She didn't know," I said quietly.

"She didn't know," Jaenelle confirmed. "Or she knew and just...didn't think about it. I don't know which is worse."

I didn't either.

"So, I told her," Jaenelle said, her voice tight. "Because your daughter has the same birthday as my sister. You can't throw Lisa a surprise party and act like your own child doesn't exist. You have to acknowledge her birthday too."

Silence stretched between us.

"What did she say?" I finally asked.

"She just looked at me for a few seconds," Jaenelle said. "Like she was trying to process it. And then she said, 'Oh. Right.' Like she'd just remembered you were born. Or like that fact hadn't even occurred to her that it might be a problem."

I pressed my hand to my chest, trying to breathe through the tightness.

"I told her the optics would be bad," Jaenelle continued. "That family and friends would notice. That people would ask why she's celebrating Lisa but not you. That it would look…really messed up."

"And?"

"She finally agreed to cancel it," Jaenelle said. "But I don't think she understood *why* it was wrong. I think she just didn't want to deal with people asking questions and judging her."

Of course.

"I'm sorry," Jaenelle said softly. "I know this is a lot. But I thought you should know before you heard it from someone else. Because if she's planning stuff like this and not even thinking about you...I don't know. I just wanted you to be aware."

"Thank you," I managed. "Really. Thank you for standing up for me."

"Always," Jaenelle said. "You're my cousin. You deserve better than this."

When I hung up, I sat on my couch—frozen in disbelief.

My coffee had gone cold.

The TV was still playing, but I couldn't hear it anymore.

All I could hear was my mother's voice in my head—not from this conversation, but from a lifetime of conversations:

"You're so ungrateful."

"I did my best."

"You don't know what I've been through."

And now: *"Why would I need two of everything?"*

She remembered Lisa's birthday.

She cared enough to plan a party—venue, cake, decorations, family.

She cared enough to FaceTime Jae and coordinate details.

She cared enough to make her niece feel special.

But her own daughter?

Born on the exact same day, just one year earlier?

Didn't even register.

Not as an afterthought.

Not as someone who might be hurt.

Just…nothing.

She didn't overlook me. She placed me exactly where I had always been.

Erased.

And the worst part?

In forty-nine years she'd never thrown me a party.

Not a surprise party.

Not a tea party.

Not even a cake with candles and a half-hearted "Happy Birthday written in icing."

Nothing.

Ever.

But Lisa? Her forty-eight year old niece?

She'd go all out.

Because Lisa mattered.

And I didn't.

I called Lisa.

"She what?" Lisa said, stunned.

I told her the whole story.

There was a long silence on the other end.

"I'm going to say something cousin," Lisa finally said. "And I need you to really hear me."

"Okay."

"Your mother has issues. It's like she doesn't see you as a daughter—as a person. I mean, how can she be so cold?"

The words landed like a punch to the chest.

"I know that sounds harsh," Lisa continued. "But it's the truth. She can show up for her sister's kids. She can show up for your brothers. She can plan and coordinate and make them feel special. She has the capacity to love, to celebrate, to care. She just doesn't extend it to you. Yeah, something's up with that."

I swallowed hard.

"And the fact that her niece had to explain to her why it would be fucked up—that she didn't instinctively realize it on her own—at her big age, tells you everything you need to know."

"Yeah," I whispered.

"This isn't about her forgetting," Lisa said. "I believe she did this intentionally. This is about you not being real to her. Yeah, she gave birth to you, but she doesn't see you as a daughter."

I wanted to argue.

But I couldn't.

Because she was right.

"I'm sorry," Lisa said, her voice softening. "I know you've been doing so much work to heal. And then she pulls this shit and it's like she won't let you have any peace."

"She won't," I said. "Even when I don't talk to her, even when I've blocked her, she still finds ways to leach into my life to remind me that I don't matter."

"But you do matter," Lisa said firmly. "You matter to me. You matter to Jaenelle. You matter to everyone who actually sees you. Your mother's inability to see you—that's her sickness. Not yours."

After we hung up, I sat in a daze at my kitchen table for a long time staring out the window.

I needed some fresh air.

I grabbed my jacket and went for a walk to ground myself.

Upon returning, I headed straight to my altar.

I didn't have a plan. I just needed to do something.

I lit a white candle.

Pulled a card.

What is this? What am I dealing with?

The card I turned over was one I'd seen before, over and over:

The Devil.

Chains. Bondage. Illusion. Being trapped in a pattern and not even knowing you're trapped.

But this time, I saw it differently.

The figure in the card—the Devil himself—wasn't holding the chains.

The people were chained, yes.

But the chains were loose.

They could slip free if they wanted to.

They just didn't realize it yet.

I stared at the card.

She's chained.

Not to me.

To the pattern. To the energy. To whatever dark force has been compelling her for lifetimes.

And she doesn't even know it.

She thinks this is just who she is.

She thinks forgetting my birthday is normal. Planning a party for her niece while excluding me is fine. Erasing me from her life while still reaching for me when it suits her—that's just how things are.

Because she's not in control.

The energy driving her is.

I pulled another card.

What do I do?

The Eight of Swords.

The woman, bound and blindfolded, surrounded by swords.

Trapped.

But the bindings are loose.

She could free herself if she realized the cage was an illusion.

I laughed—a bitter, exhausted sound.

"I get it," I said aloud. "She's trapped. I can see that. But I'm not the one who can free her. She has to do that herself."

I set the cards down.

And I made a decision.

I wasn't going to call her.

I wasn't going to confront her about the party.

I wasn't going to explain, again, why what she did was hurtful.

Because it wouldn't matter. It never mattered.

She wouldn't hear me.

Something wouldn't let her.

But I also realized something else:

I needed to find out more.

The New Orleans session had shown me how she controls, how she refuses to let go.

But I still didn't understand why.

Why was the pattern so relentless?

Why couldn't she just leave me alone?

Why did she keep pursuing me, hurting me, taunting me, erasing me—over and over and over?

There had to be more.

More lifetimes. More betrayals. More pieces of the puzzle.

And I needed to see them.

Not to save her.

But to understand the full scope of what I was dealing with.

So I could finally, completely, break free.

I texted Pam:

"Can we move my next session up? Something happened. I'm ready to go deeper."

Her response came within minutes:

"Yes. Let's do this Friday. 2 p.m. Virtual again?"

"Yes. Thank you."

I set my phone down and looked at the cards still laid out on my altar.

The Devil. The Eight of Swords.

Bondage. Illusion. The belief that you're trapped when the door is actually open.

She's trapped, I thought. But I'm not.

And I'm going to prove it.

CHAPTER 8
The Color Line (South Carolina)

Friday came faster than I expected.

I'd spent the week since Jaenelle's phone call in a fog—going through the motions, working, pretending I was fine while my mother's voice echoed in my head: "Why would I need two of everything?"

By the time I logged into Zoom at 1:55 p.m., I was ready.

Ready to go deeper.

Ready to understand why erasure felt so familiar.

Pam's face appeared on the screen, and she studied me for a moment before speaking.

"How are you?" she asked.

"Angry," I said. "And tired of being angry."

She nodded. "Good. Let's use that. Anger is clarity. It cuts through the bullshit and shows you what's real."

She leaned forward slightly.

"You said something happened. You want to tell me about it before we go under?"

I told her about the birthday party. About my mother planning to celebrate Lisa and forgetting I existed. About Jae having to explain why that was wrong.

Pam's expression didn't change, but I saw something flicker in her eyes—recognition, maybe. Or just deep, practiced, heartfelt compassion for how cruel mothers could be.

"She erased you," Pam said simply.

"Yeah."

"And that's not the first time."

"No."

Pam sat back. "Okay. So, here's what I'm sensing. The lifetime that's coming up next—I feel it's going to show you another flavor of erasure. Not the grooming and control you saw in New Orleans. Something else. Something about choices. About a mother who had to choose, and didn't pick you."

My chest tightened.

"Are you ready?" Pam asked.

I nodded.

"Then let's begin."

Going Under

Pam guided me through the familiar process—breathing, relaxation, sinking deeper.

"I want you to go back to the lifetime that's been calling you since the birthday party incident. The one that wants to be seen. Let it come into focus."

My breathing slowed.

The room around me faded.

And then—

Heat.

Not the hot, sticky, oppressive heat of New Orleans.

This was different. Dry. Heavy. The kind of heat that sat on your skin like a weight and made everything feel slower, harder, more exhausting.

I smelled earth. Sweat. Lye soap.

And I heard voices—low, careful, the kind of voices people use when they're always afraid someone's listening.

South Carolina. 1913

I am ten years old.

My name—in this life—is Ruth.

I live in a small house on the edge of a town I don't know the name of. The house is wood, unpainted, with gaps in the boards that let the wind through in winter. We have three rooms. A main room with a table and a stove. A back room where my mother sleeps. And a loft where I sleep, reached by a ladder.

It's just the two of us.

My mother's name is Cora.

And she is beautiful.

Not in the way I am beautiful—because I am not. I know this already, at ten years old, because people have told me.

My mother is light-skinned. Her hair is long, soft, wavy. Her eyes are green. When she walks through town, white men look at her. Black men look at her. Everyone looks at her.

I am dark.

My skin is the color of wet earth. My hair is short, coarse, thick, and hard to manage. My nose is wide. My lips are full.

I look like my father.

And my father is gone.

"Tell me about your mother," Pam's voice said, distant but grounding.

"She's trying to survive," I said. "That's all she cares about. Surviving."

"And you?"

"I'm…in the way."

My mother works for a white family in town. The Harrisons.

She cleans their house, cooks their meals, washes their clothes. She's good at it. Quiet. Obedient. She knows how to make herself small, how to smile without showing her teeth, how to say "yes, ma'am" and "no, sir" in a way that makes white people comfortable.

They like her.

Mrs. Harrison especially.

"Cora is so refined," I've heard her say. "Not like the others. She's got…breeding."

What Mrs. Harrison means is: She's almost white.

And my mother knows it.

She uses it.

I don't go to the Harrison house.

My mother doesn't take me.

"You stay here," she tells me every morning before she leaves. "Clean the house. Fetch water. Stay out of sight."

I know why.

Because if the Harrisons see me—if they see how dark I am, how much I look like the man my mother won't talk about—they'll know.

They'll know she's not "refined."

They'll know she's just like everyone else.

And she'll lose her position.

There's a man who comes around sometimes.

Mr. Pritchard.

He's white. Middle-aged. Owns a store in town.

He looks at my mother the way men look at things they want to own.

And my mother lets him.

Not because she wants to.

But because he has money. Because he can help her. Because survival isn't about dignity—it's about making it to tomorrow.

One day, when I'm ten, Mr. Pritchard comes to the house while I'm there.

I'm in the back room, folding clothes, when I hear his voice in the main room.

"Cora," he says, his voice slow and syrupy. "I've been thinking."

"Yes, sir?" my mother says, and I can hear the smile in her voice. The performed sweetness.

"I could help you," he says. "Set you up proper. A real house. In town. You wouldn't have to work for the Harrisons anymore."

A pause.

"That's very kind of you, Mr. Pritchard," my mother says carefully.

"Of course," he continues, "there'd be…conditions."

Another pause.

"What kind of conditions?" my mother asks, though I think she already knows.

"Well," he says, and I can hear the grin in his voice. "You'd be my girl. You understand? You'd keep house for me. And…well. You know."

I hear my mother take a breath.

"I understand," she says.

"Good," he says. "There's just one thing."

"What's that?"

"The child," he says. "She can't come."

Silence.

My heart stops.

"She's dark," Mr. Pritchard continues, his voice casual, like he's discussing livestock. "People would talk. They'd wonder. It wouldn't look right, you understand."

More silence.

"So if you want this arrangement," he says, "you'll have to…make other plans for her."

I hold my breath, waiting for my mother to say no.

Waiting for her to defend me.

Waiting for her to choose me.

"What does she say?" Pam's voice asked with compassion.

I felt tears on my face.

"She says yes."

My mother says yes.

Not right away.

She says, "Let me think about it."

But I know.

I already know.

Because I've seen the way she looks at me.

Like I'm a problem.

Like I'm the thing standing between her and the life she wants.

Three days later, my mother tells me.

We're sitting at the table, eating cornbread and beans, and she says it so casually I almost don't register the words at first.

"You're going to live with Aunt Ida Mae for a while."

I look up. "What?"

"Aunt Ida Mae," my mother repeats, not looking at me. "Down in the country. She's got a farm. She needs help. And I…I've got an opportunity. In town."

"What opportunity?" I ask, even though I already know.

"A position," she says. "A good one. But I can't take you with me."

"Why not?"

She finally looks at me, and there's no softness in her eyes.

"Because it's not appropriate," she says. "You'll be better off with Aunt Ida Mae. She'll take care of you."

"I don't want to go," I say, my voice small.

"It's not about what you want," my mother says, her voice hardening. "It's about survival. And right now, I need to survive."

"And you?" Pam's voice asked. "What about you surviving?"

"I don't matter," I said, the words scraping out of my throat. "She made that clear."

I'm sent away a week later.

Aunt Ida Mae lives three hours away by wagon, in a rural area where the roads are dirt and the houses are even smaller than ours.

She's not really my aunt. She's some distant relative, or maybe just a woman my mother knows who agreed to take me in exchange for free labor.

She's not cruel.

But she's not kind either.

She feeds me. Gives me a place to sleep. Works me from sunrise to sunset—cleaning, cooking, hauling water, tending animals.

And I wait.

Wait for my mother to come back.

Wait for her to change her mind.

Wait for her to realize she made a mistake.

She never comes.

Not once.

Not for my birthday. Not for Christmas. Not ever.

I hear about her sometimes, through people who pass through. Word travels, even in small towns.

I hear she's living in a house in town now. A nice house. With Mr. Pritchard.

I hear she's doing well.

I hear she looks happy.

And I realize: she didn't just send me away to survive.

She sent me away because I was evidence.

Evidence that she wasn't as light, as refined, as acceptable as she wanted people to believe.

I was the dark-skinned daughter who reminded everyone where she really came from.

And she erased me. Just like that.

I die at fourteen.

Not all at once. Slowly.

Consumption, they call it. A nasty cough that never left me. My body kept giving and giving, until there was nothing left to give.

Aunt Ida Mae says I'm weak. Says I don't eat enough. Says everybody's tired.

No one notices that I am disappearing.

And when I finally stop breathing, it feels less like dying and more like finishing something that had already been decided.

Aunt Ida Mae buries me in the back field, near the other graves of people whose names no one remembers.

My mother doesn't come to the funeral.

I don't know if she even knows I'm dead.

Or if she does, if she cares.

As my soul lifts from that body, I look back one last time.

At the life I didn't get to live.

At the mother who chose proximity to whiteness over her own child.

At the pattern I've been trapped in for lifetimes.

And I understand something I didn't before:

She didn't reject me because I was bad.

She rejected me because I was inconvenient.

Because loving me would cost her something.

And she wasn't willing to pay.

I came back to the present gasping, tears streaming down my face.

Pam was there, on the screen, her face calm and steady.

"Welcome back," she said softly. "Take your time."

I couldn't speak.

My chest was tight, my throat raw, my whole body shaking.

"What did you see?" Pam asked softly.

I told her.

All of it.

South Carolina. My mother Cora. Mr. Pritchard. Being sent away because I was too dark, too much of a reminder, too inconvenient.

Dying at fourteen, alone, forgotten.

When I finished, Pam was quiet for a moment.

"Do you see the pattern?" she asked.

I nodded, wiping my face.

"She chose herself," I said. "She chose survival. She chose what would make her life easier. And I was the cost."

"Yes," Pam said. "And in this lifetime?"

I thought about the birthday party.

About my mother planning to celebrate Lisa and forgetting I

existed.

About the email. The text. The lifetime of erasure.

"She's still doing it," I whispered. "She's still choosing herself. Still erasing me. Still acting like I'm inconvenient."

"Yes," Pam said. "That's the pattern."

Clearing

Before we ended, Pam guided me through a clearing.

"Close your eyes," she said. "Check your heart space."

I did.

The room in my heart was darker than it had been after New Orleans.

There was a shadow in the corner—shame, thick and heavy.

"I see shame," I said.

"Whose shame?" Pam asked.

I paused.

"Hers," I realized. "It's not mine. It's hers. She was ashamed of me. Ashamed of what I represented."

"Good," Pam said. "Now I want you to pick that shame up and hand it back to her. It's not yours to carry."

I imagined myself lifting the shadow—heavy, sticky,

suffocating.

And I set it down outside the room.

"This is yours," I said aloud. "Not mine."

The room in my heart lightened immediately.

Closing

"You did beautiful work today," Pam said. "That was one of the hardest lifetimes to witness—not because of physical violence, but because of the soul violence. The erasure. The being chosen against."

"Yeah," I said, my voice hoarse.

"And you survived it," Pam continued. "You survived her choosing herself over you. You survived being erased. And you're here now, remembering, so you can finally let it go."

I nodded.

"Rest," Pam said. "Journal if you need to. We'll talk in a few weeks about the next session."

After we ended the call, I drank a glass of water and lied down on my bed to relax and think.

Later, I got up, grabbed my cards and pulled one.

What do I need to know after today?

The card that flipped up was the **Two of Swords**.

A woman, blindfolded, holding two swords crossed over her

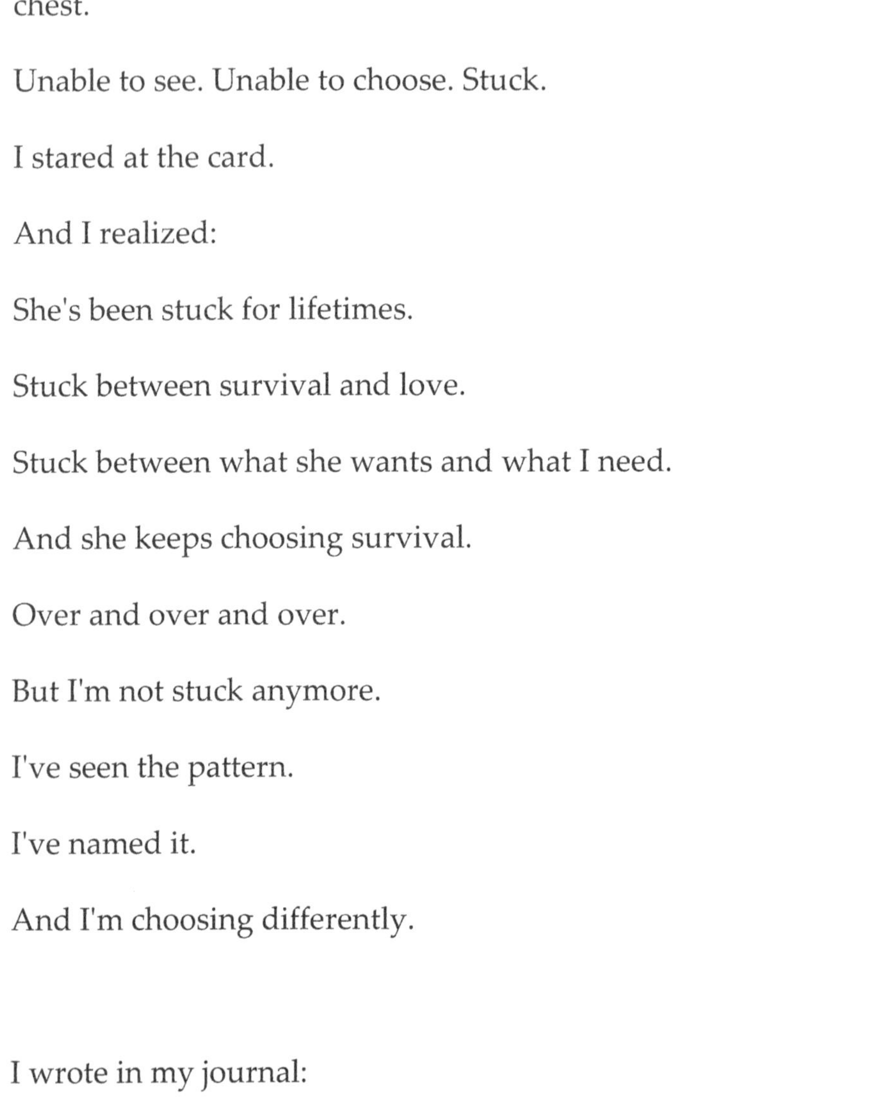

chest.

Unable to see. Unable to choose. Stuck.

I stared at the card.

And I realized:

She's been stuck for lifetimes.

Stuck between survival and love.

Stuck between what she wants and what I need.

And she keeps choosing survival.

Over and over and over.

But I'm not stuck anymore.

I've seen the pattern.

I've named it.

And I'm choosing differently.

I wrote in my journal:

South Carolina, 1913: She chose whiteness over me. Chose proximity to power. Chose survival at the cost of her own child.

New Orleans, 1891: She chose profit over me. Chose control. Chose to own me rather than love me.

Egypt, 1320 BCE: She chose duty over me. Chose her gods, her status, her position.

This life, 2026: She chose everyone else over me. Her niece. Her image. Her comfort. What made her happy.

Same pattern. Different costumes.

She keeps choosing herself.

And I keep paying the price.

But not anymore.

I set the pen down and looked at my altar.

The candles had burned down.

The incense had gone out.

But I felt something shifting.

Not healing yet. But clarity. Cold, sharp, undeniable clarity.

I knew what I was dealing with now.

And I was ready to go deeper down the rabbit hole.

CHAPTER 9
The Ancestors

Two months passed before I saw Pam again.

Not because I wasn't ready.

But because I needed time.

Time to let South Carolina settle into my bones. Time to understand what I'd seen. Time to stop asking why and start asking what now.

The first week after the session, I could barely function.

I'd wake up and feel the weight of Cora's shame pressing down on my chest—that thick, suffocating feeling of being inconvenient. Of being the thing that stood between someone and the life they wanted.

I'd look in the mirror and see Ruth's face—dark-skinned, wide-nosed, the daughter who was too much evidence, too much reminder, too much problem.

And I'd have to remind myself:

That was then. This is now. I'm not her anymore.

But some days, I didn't believe it.

The second week, something shifted.

I started feeling them.

Not just my grandmother—though she was there, always, a steady presence in the background.

But others.

Women I didn't know but somehow recognized.

I'd be cooking dinner and feel someone standing beside me, watching.

I'd be at my altar and sense a crowd gathering—silent, patient, waiting.

I'd wake up in the middle of the night and know, without seeing, that I wasn't alone in the room.

It should have scared me.

But it didn't.

Because they didn't feel threatening.

They felt...expectant.

Like they'd been waiting for something.

Or someone.

By the third week, I started venerating them intentionally.

It wasn't something I planned. It just felt...necessary.

On Sunday, I cooked a full dinner the way my grandmother used to—fried cabbage, cornbread, baked chicken, macaroni and cheese. The kind of meal that takes all day to cook and fills the house with the smell of home.

When it was done, I set the table.

But I didn't sit down to eat.

Instead, I took a small plate—one of my grandmother's old dishes, the bone China with the tiny blue flower design around the edge—and filled it. A little bit of everything.

I carried it to my altar and set it down carefully, next to the candles and the cowrie shells and my grandmother's photo.

"This is for you." I said aloud, feeling a deep certainty. "For all of you. The mothers and daughters. The ones who came before. The ones who couldn't break free."

I lit a white candle.

"I see you," I whispered. "And I'm listening."

The next day, I went to the botanica and bought ancestor money—the kind with gold foil, printed with blessings and symbols I didn't fully understand but felt drawn to anyway.

I came home and set up outside on my small patio.

I placed the money in a metal bowl, struck a match, and watched it burn.

The flames caught quickly, curling the joss paper, turning it to ash.

And as it burned, I spoke:

"This is for you. For your comfort. For your peace. For whatever you need on the other side."

Something about this always feels right.

And when the last of the paper turned to ash and the smoke drifted up into the sky, I felt something loosen in my chest.

Like an exhale I'd been holding for lifetimes.

That night, I dreamed.

But it wasn't a past life.

It was my grandmother.

She was sitting in her kitchen—the one I remembered from childhood, with the yellow curtains and the smell of coffee always lingering in the air.

She was smiling.

"There you are," she said, like she'd been waiting.

I sat down across from her, and even though I knew this was a dream, it felt real.

More real than waking.

"Grandma," I said, my voice thick. "I don't know what I'm doing."

"Yes, you do," she said lovingly. "You're doing exactly what you're supposed to be doing."

"It hurts," I said.

"I know, baby. I know."

She reached across the table and took my hand.

"But it's not going to hurt forever," she said. "You're almost there. You're seeing it now. The whole picture. And once you see it—really see it—you can let it go."

I wanted to believe her.

"Why me?" I asked, the question I'd been carrying for weeks. "Why do I have to be the one who sees all this? Why can't she just…be different?"

My grandmother's expression softened.

"Because she can't," she said simply. "She's trapped, baby. Been trapped for longer than you know. And you—" She squeezed my hand. "You're the one who's strong enough to break free. Not just for you. For all of us."

I stared at her.

"What do you mean, all of us?"

She gestured behind her, and suddenly I saw them.

Other women.

Standing in the doorway. Filling the kitchen. Crowding the hallway beyond.

Faces I didn't recognize but somehow knew.

My ancestors.

The mothers and daughters of my line, stretching back through time.

Some of them looked tired. Some looked sad. Some looked angry.

But all of them were looking at me.

"They couldn't do it," my grandmother said softly. "We tried. But the wound was too deep. The pattern too strong. We didn't have the tools. Didn't have the knowledge. Didn't have the strength. Thank God—it only grazed me."

She looked at me, and her eyes were full of something I'd never seen before.

Pride.

"But you do," she said. "You see it clearly. You have the rage we were too scared to feel. You have the tools we didn't have. And you have the courage to do what we couldn't."

One of the women stepped forward—older, her face lined with years I couldn't count, her eyes ancient.

She looked at me for a long moment.

And then she spoke, her voice low and steady:

"I'm sorry you had to carry this. But you're the only one who can end it."

I woke up crying, my face drenched with tears.

The dream was already fading, but the feeling of it remained—heavy, urgent, undeniable.

I sat up in bed, my heart pounding—

You're the only one who can end it.

I stumbled out of bed and went to my altar.

The plate of food I'd left was still there, untouched—but somehow it looked different. Felt different—Lighter. Like something had been taken from it, even if the physical food still remained.

I lit a candle with shaking hands.

And I reached for my Ancestor Oracle Deck—the one I saved for the deepest questions, the ones I couldn't ask the tarot.

I shuffled, hands trembling.

"Is it true?" I whispered. "Am I the one? Am I supposed to end this?"

I pulled a card.

The Healer.

I pulled another.

The Breaker of Chains.

And another.

The Chosen One.

I stared at the cards, holding my breath.

And then I pulled one more.

The card that came up had a single phrase written across it in bold letters:

"You are the one we've been waiting for."

I sat back, the cards spread in front of me, my whole body trembling.

Not with fear.

With recognition.

Because I'd known, hadn't I?

On some level, I'd always known.

That's why the past lives kept coming.

That's why I couldn't let it go, couldn't just "forgive and move on" the way everyone told me to.

That's why I'd been doing this work—the regressions, the divination, the rituals.

Because I wasn't just healing myself.

I was healing the line.

All the mothers and daughters who came before me.

All the ones who would come after.

I was the one chosen to see it.

To name it.

To break it.

I pulled out my journal and wrote:

The ancestors came to me in a dream. My grandmother and the others. They told me I was chosen. Not to suffer. Not to be punished. But to end this. To break the curse that's been running through the bloodline for generations.

I pulled cards. They confirmed it.

I am the Healer.

I am the Breaker of Chains.

I am the Chosen One.

This pain I've been carrying—it's not random. It's not punishment. It's preparation.

I was meant to see all of this so I could be strong enough to end it.

And I will.

I set the pen down and looked at the cards still laid out on my altar.

The Healer. The Breaker of Chains. The Chosen One.

"Okay," I said aloud, my voice steady now. "I hear you. I understand."

I took a breath.

"I'm ready."

The next morning, I texted Pam:

"I need to schedule the next session. There's one more past life I think I need to see before I can do the deeper work. I'm ready."

She responded within the hour:

"I was wondering when you'd reach out. I've had a feeling you were

close. Let's do this Monday, 2 p.m. Virtual?"

"Yes. Thank you."

I set my phone down and looked at my altar one more time.

The ancestors were quiet now.

But I could feel them.

Watching.

Waiting.

Trusting me to do what they couldn't.

And I wasn't going to let them down.

CHAPTER 10
Blue Notes (New York)

Two months had passed since South Carolina.

Two months of processing what I had learned—

about colorism, about being overlooked, about not being chosen, about what was never mine to carry. Two months of watching my dreams shift again—

No longer the dry heat of the South.

But something different.

Urban. Electric. Alive with music.

I could hear it before I could see it.

The low thrum of a bass.

The bright brassy timbre of a trumpet.

And a voice—

Smooth.

Sultry.

Aching.

Singing about love and loss and longing in a way that made your chest hurt.

And there she was—

Again.

Friday 2 p.m.

I logged into Zoom.

Pam's face appeared on the screen, calm and steady.

"How are you feeling?" she asked.

"Ready," I said. "Whatever this is, I'm ready."

She nodded. "Good. Let's go."

Going Under

She guided me into the trance—breathing, sinking, letting go.

"I want you to go back to the 1930s. To Harlem. To the lifetime that's been calling you. Let it come into focus."

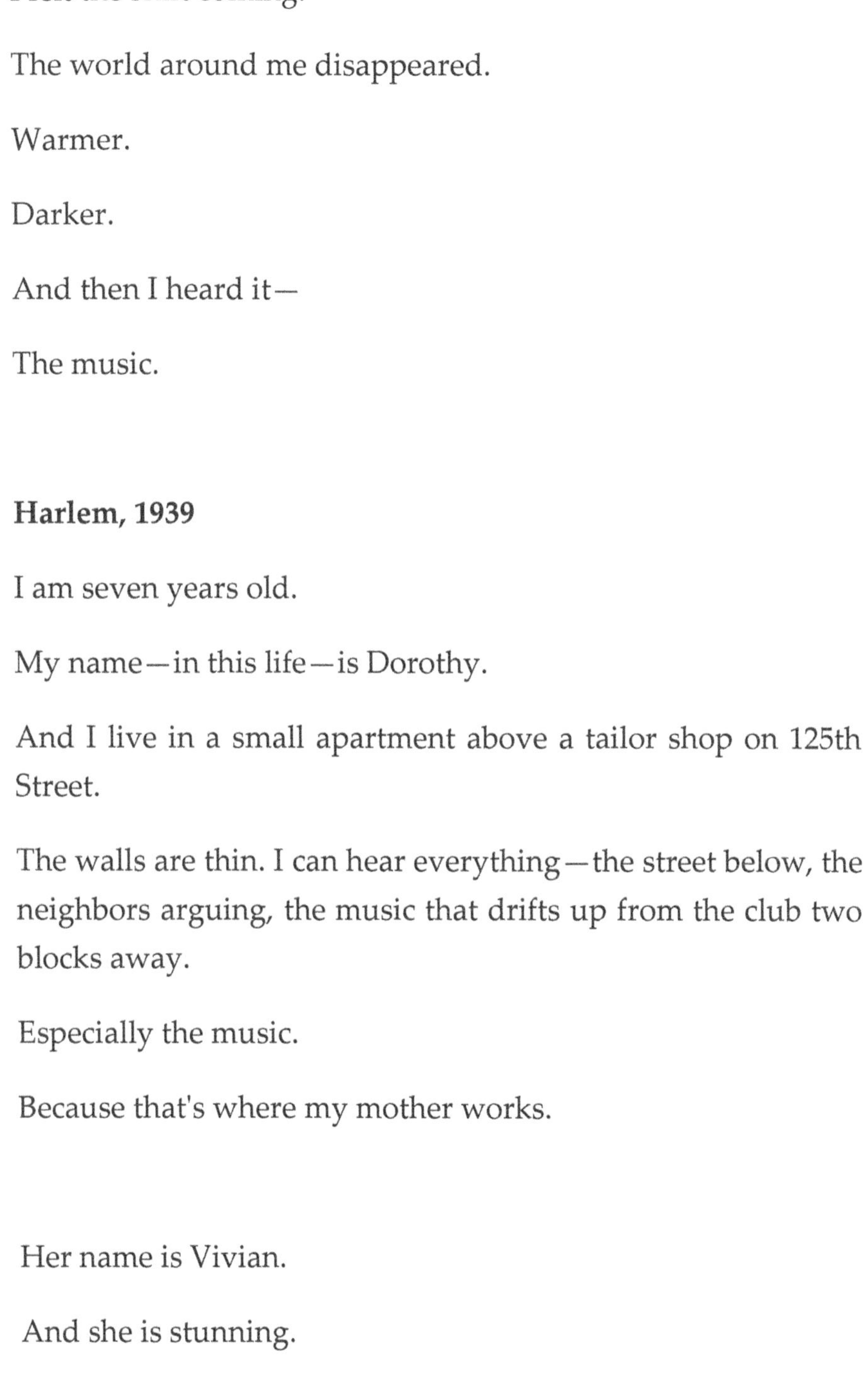

I felt the shift coming.

The world around me disappeared.

Warmer.

Darker.

And then I heard it—

The music.

Harlem, 1939

I am seven years old.

My name—in this life—is Dorothy.

And I live in a small apartment above a tailor shop on 125th Street.

The walls are thin. I can hear everything—the street below, the neighbors arguing, the music that drifts up from the club two blocks away.

Especially the music.

Because that's where my mother works.

Her name is Vivian.

And she is stunning.

Not just pretty—beautiful in a way that stops people mid-stride.

High cheekbones. Copper skin that glows even in dim light. Eyes like dark honey. Her hair in finger waves that frame her face like a painting.

And her voice—

God, her voice.

Low and rich and full of something I can't name yet but will later recognize as longing.

She sings at the Blue Note, a club where Black folks go to forget their troubles for a few hours.

She's not the headliner.

Not yet.

But she will be, she says.

Soon.

"I'm gonna be somebody," she tells me, fixing her makeup in the cracked mirror by the door. "You watch. One day, people are gonna know my name."

I watch her get ready every night.

The ritual of it—the lipstick applied just so, the dress that hugs her curves, the perfume she dabs at her wrists and throat.

She transforms.

At home, she's tired. Quiet. Sometimes sharp-tongued.

But when she's dressed for the stage, she's someone else.

Someone powerful.

Someone who matters.

"Who's watching you tonight?" she asks, not looking at me.

"Mrs. Calloway," I say. The neighbor downstairs.

"Good. Be good for her. And don't wait up."

She's gone before I can say goodnight.

I don't know my father.

I know his name—Johnny B.

I know he played trumpet.

I know he left before I was born.

And I know my mother doesn't like to talk about him.

But sometimes, late at night when she's had too much to drink, she does.

"He was supposed to be different," she says, staring at nothing. "He told me we were going places. That we'd make it together.

Him on trumpet, me singing. We'd be a duo. The next big thing."

She laughs, bitter.

"Then I got knocked up. And he got gone."

I learn early not to ask questions.

Not to cry when she snaps at me.

Not to need too much.

Because needing things makes her angry.

And when she's angry, she reminds me:

"You know what I gave up for you?"

"Tell me what you're experiencing," Pam said, her voice keeping me anchored.

"I'm a child," I said. "Maybe seven. My mother is a singer. She's beautiful. Talented. But she's…bitter. And I'm the reason."

"Stay with it. What happens next?"

The years pass.

I get older—ten, twelve, fourteen.

And my mother gets…harder.

The club doesn't love her the way it used to.

Younger women rotate through the spotlight like fresh promises.

Girls with brighter smiles, higher voices, bodies that haven't been worn down by disappointment yet.

My mother still sings—but later now. Shorter sets. Fewer tips.

She tells herself it's temporary.

That real recognition is just around the corner.

But I can see it in her eyes:

She's starting to realize it's not coming.

At home, I learn how to disappear.

I make my own food when there is food.

I keep quiet when men come through the door—musicians, gamblers, men who smell like whiskey and promises they won't keep.

I sit very still when she practices, afraid my breathing might pull her out of whatever world she goes to when she sings.

Sometimes she looks at me—really looks.

Not with hatred.

With calculation.

One night, after a show that didn't go the way she wanted, she pours herself a drink and sits across from me at the table.

The room smells like gin and disappointment.

The radio played low in the background—Duke Ellington.

She studies my face for a long time.

"You know," she says slowly, "you got his eyes."

I freeze.

She's never said his name to me before.

Johnny B has been a ghost in this house for years.

"I gave up a lot," she continues, not unkindly. "People don't understand that. They think women just…end up places. They don't see the choices."

She takes a sip of her drink.

"I could've been something."

The sentence hangs there, unfinished.

Then she looks at me again—really looks this time—and something in her settles.

Not grief.

Not regret.

Decision.

From that night on, she treats me like *proof.*

Every failure becomes my fault.

Every missed opportunity, my shadow.

When she drinks, she reminds me of what she lost.

When she's sober, she reminds me to stay out of the way.

I am not abused.

Not in the way people think of abuse.

She doesn't hit me. Doesn't scream.

But she blots me out.

When men at the club notice me—"Your daughter's getting pretty, Viv"—she shuts it down fast.

"She ain't nothing special."

When teachers compliment my intelligence—"Dorothy's a bright girl, real smart"—she dismisses it.

"Book smart don't mean nothing in the real world."

When I sing—softly, once, when I think she isn't listening—she tells me to stop.

"That voice," she says harshly. "Don't do that."

I understand then.

She doesn't want me gone.

She wants me smaller than her regret.

"How does that make you feel?" Pam asked softly.

"Like suffocation," I said, tears streaming down my face. "Like I'm not allowed to be anything she couldn't be. Like my existence is proof of her failure."

"Very good. Keep going."

Years pass.

I turn sixteen. Seventeen. Eighteen.

And I start to plan.

I save what little money I can from odd jobs—cleaning, mending clothes, running errands.

I keep my head down.

And I wait.

When I'm old enough to leave—nineteen, maybe twenty—I pack my things.

One suitcase. Everything I own fits inside it.

My mother watches from the doorway, arms folded, face unreadable.

She doesn't stop me.

Doesn't ask where I'm going.

Just watches.

At the door, I turn back.

This is the moment—

The one children carry in their bones forever.

The last chance for something to shift.

For her to say Wait, or I'm sorry, or I love you.

"Mama," I say, my voice barely above a whisper. "Did you ever love me?"

She doesn't hesitate.

Doesn't soften.

Doesn't look away.

"I loved the life I was supposed to have."

That's it.

No cruelty in her voice.

No drama.

Just truth delivered straight—no chaser.

As cold and clear as a bell.

I turn.

Walk down the stairs.

Step out onto 125th Street.

And something inside me cracks—

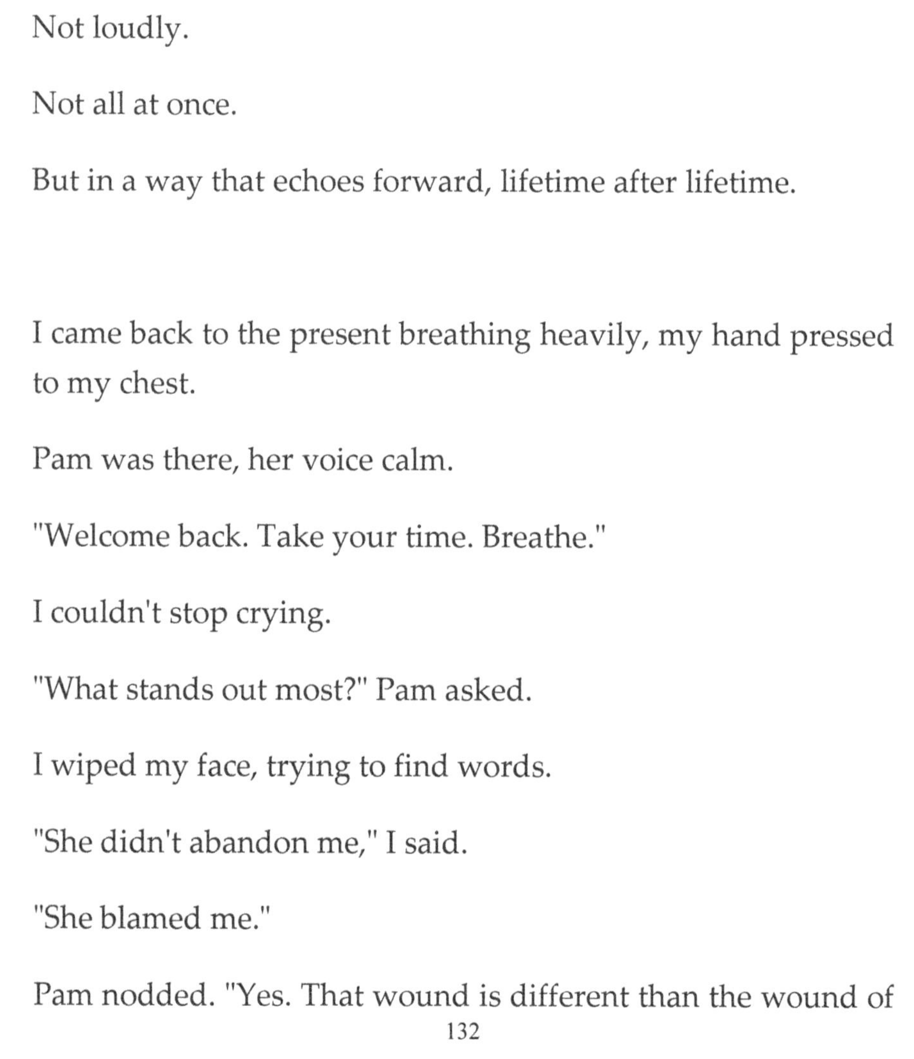

Not loudly.

Not all at once.

But in a way that echoes forward, lifetime after lifetime.

I came back to the present breathing heavily, my hand pressed to my chest.

Pam was there, her voice calm.

"Welcome back. Take your time. Breathe."

I couldn't stop crying.

"What stands out most?" Pam asked.

I wiped my face, trying to find words.

"She didn't abandon me," I said.

"She blamed me."

Pam nodded. "Yes. That wound is different than the wound of

abandonment."

"She kept me close," I continued, the realization settling in. "She fed me. Housed me. Watched me grow. But she made me the living proof of everything she hated about herself."

"Yes."

"And that—" My voice broke. "That's a betrayal that haunts you long after you leave the room."

Clearing

"Let's do some clearing work. Close your eyes." Pam said.

I did.

"Check your heart space. Look inside. What do you see?"

I turned my awareness inward.

The space in my heart was dim.

Heavy.

And in the center was a mirror—cracked, distorted, reflecting an image I didn't recognize.

"I see a broken mirror," I said.

"That's her perception of you," Pam said. "Not the truth. I want you to take that mirror and shatter it completely. You don't need to see yourself through her eyes anymore."

I imagined my hands gripping the mirror.

And I threw it to the ground.

It shattered into a thousand pieces.

And underneath—

Light.

Pure, clear light.

The space in my heart flooded with it.

"Good," Pam said softly. "That's you. That's who you truly are. Not her regret. Not her failure. Just the real you."

Closing

"Listen to me," Pam said. "We've been calling this energy a pattern based on its behavior. But when a pattern organizes itself across generations with this kind of precision? That's different. That's a generational curse at work. And a curse isn't always a spirit. In lots of cases, it's a spoken or energetic condition that keeps recreating the same outcome until someone interrupts it."

I didn't flinch.

I knew she was right.

"Let this integrate," Pam continued. "You're at the threshold now. The original wound is close. Pay attention to what comes up. Remember to be gentle with yourself."

"Do you think I need another session?" I asked.

Pam paused, considering.

"No," she said. "You've seen enough to know that the pattern is the mechanism of the curse. What's left is understanding the origin so you can break it. And I have a feeling that's going to come to you outside of hypnosis. In a dream, maybe. Or a revelation. The ancestors will show you when you're ready." "You've seen how it moves," she said. "Now you need to see where it began. "

After the call ended, I sat with my thoughts for a long time.

I felt emptied. Like I had been given a spiritual enema. But also… clear. Crystal clear.

Then it occurred to me—

The pattern wasn't just about cruelty, rejection, shame, or abandonment. It was about blame.

About mothers who could not separate their daughters from their own disappointments.

About women who held their children close—and slowly, quietly, passed down resentment instead of healing.

This had happened before in the lineage. Through different women with the same wound.

Across lifetimes.

Like a soul unwilling to release what no longer served her.

Unwilling to loosen her grip on grievance.

Pam was right. This was a generational curse.

I pulled a card from my ancestor oracle deck.

What do I need to know after today?

The card read:

"You are closer than you think."

I set it on my altar next to the others—The Healer, The Breaker of Chains, The Chosen One, You are the one we've been waiting for.

And I whispered to the ancestors I felt gathered around me:

"Thank you for showing me. Thank you for trusting me with this. I'm ready. Show me the source. And I'll end it. I promise."

The candle on my altar flickered.

And somewhere, I felt my grandmother smile.

.

CHAPTER 11
The Mantle

Three weeks passed after the Harlem session.

Three weeks of rest, of integration, of letting the weight of 1939 settle into my bones and then slowly, carefully, release.

I followed Pam's instructions: I rested. I journaled. I did gentle clearing work. I tended my altar and fed my ancestors and let myself not push for once.

And surprisingly—miraculously—I felt...good.

Stronger.

Better than I had in months.

My anxiety, which had been a constant reminder in the background of my life for as long as I could remember, had quieted to almost nothing.

I slept through the night.

I woke up without dread sitting on my chest.

I moved through my days with a lightness I didn't know was possible.

It felt like the release was already happening, even though I hadn't done the final ritual yet.

Like the ancestors were holding me, preparing me, giving me a moment to breathe before the deepest work began.

It was a Saturday afternoon when I decided to clean my apartment.

Not because I needed to.

But because I had energy—the kind I hadn't felt in years. The kind that made me want to move, to organize, to create order in my external world now that my internal world was finally starting to clear.

I started in the bedroom, pulling things out of the closet, sorting through boxes I hadn't opened in years.

Old clothes. Books I'd forgotten I owned. Journals from my twenties filled with poems and rants and prayers I barely recognized as mine.

And then—

A box—a forgotten repository full of memories.

Taped. Dusty. Tucked in the back corner of the top shelf.

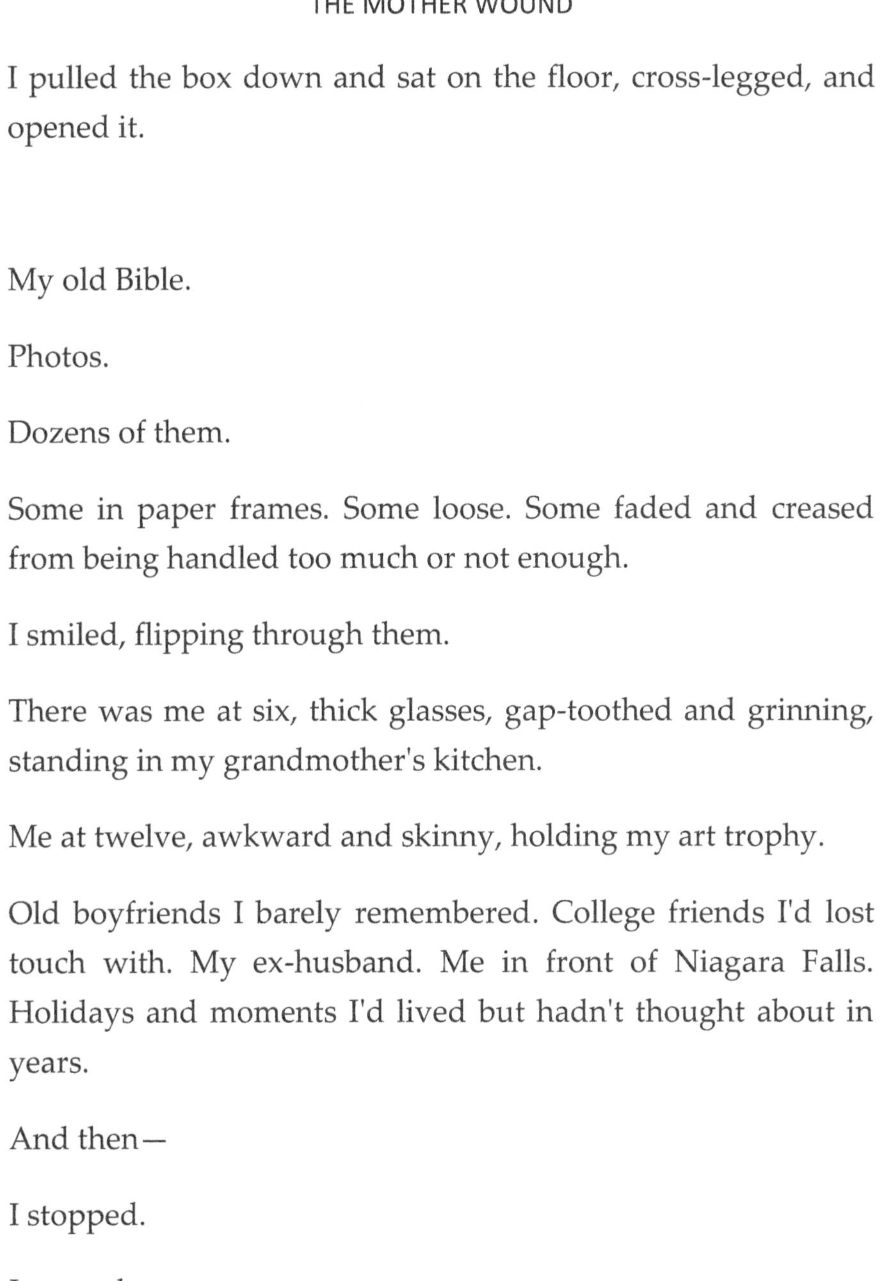

I pulled the box down and sat on the floor, cross-legged, and opened it.

My old Bible.

Photos.

Dozens of them.

Some in paper frames. Some loose. Some faded and creased from being handled too much or not enough.

I smiled, flipping through them.

There was me at six, thick glasses, gap-toothed and grinning, standing in my grandmother's kitchen.

Me at twelve, awkward and skinny, holding my art trophy.

Old boyfriends I barely remembered. College friends I'd lost touch with. My ex-husband. Me in front of Niagara Falls. Holidays and moments I'd lived but hadn't thought about in years.

And then—

I stopped.

I gasped.

It was a picture of my grandmother.

Taken just a few weeks before she died.

She was sitting in her favorite chair—the one by the window, where the afternoon light always hit just right. She was wearing a white turban on her head and her blue housecoat, the one with the flowers on it.

She looked tired.

But she was smiling.

That soft, knowing smile she always had. Like she was in on a joke the rest of us hadn't figured out yet. She was ready to go.

I stared at the photo, and suddenly I was back there.

Not in the room with her.

But on the phone.

That last phone call.

It had been a Thursday afternoon.

I'd called her just to check in, the way I always did. We talked about nothing and everything—what I'd cooked for dinner, what she was watching on TV, whether I'd heard from this cousin or that aunt.

We were laughing about something—I don't even remember what—when she said it.

"I want you to take care of this family."

The words came out of nowhere.

No preamble. No context.

Just: *I want you to take care of this family.*

I stopped laughing.

"What do you mean, Mama?"

"You heard me," she said, and there was something in her voice I didn't recognize at first. Authority. Finality. Like she was giving me an order, not making a request.

"Take-care-of-this-family," she repeated with precision.

I fumbled for a response.

"Um, how am I supposed to do that?" I asked, half-joking, half-serious. "They don't listen to me as it is. I am the black sheep, remember?"

"You heard what I said," she replied, her voice firm.

And that was it.

She moved on to another topic—something about a recipe, or the weather, or an episode of the Golden Girls that made her laugh.

And I let it go.

Because I didn't understand.

But sitting there on my bedroom floor, looking at her photo, staring at her face—

It clicked.

She wasn't asking me to mediate family drama.

She wasn't asking me to keep in touch with everyone or organize reunions or play peacemaker.

She was passing me the mantle.

The spiritual authority.

The responsibility.

She was telling me: You're the one. You're the one who's going to do the work I couldn't finish. You're the one who's going to set them free.

I pressed the photo to my chest and let the tears come.

Not sad tears.

Grateful tears.

Overwhelmed tears.

Because she'd known.

Even then, years before I started this work, before I knew about past lives or generational curses—

She'd known.

She'd seen something in me.

Recognized something.

And she'd chosen me.

I thought about all the times she'd protected me.

The way she'd come for me when I was nine days old, unwanted.

The way she'd raised me as her own, never once making me feel like a burden.

The way she'd taught me to read the cowrie shells, to trust my intuition, to see beyond what was visible.

The way she'd told me, over and over: "Don't go empty. You stay here. Don't go somewhere you can't come back from."

She'd been preparing me.

Training me.

Even when I didn't know that's what she was doing.

And that phone call—

That was her final instruction.

Her commissioning.

Take care of this family.

Not the people.

The *bloodline.*

The mothers and daughters who'd been trapped in this cycle for generations.

The ones who came before.

The ones who would come after.

Set them free.

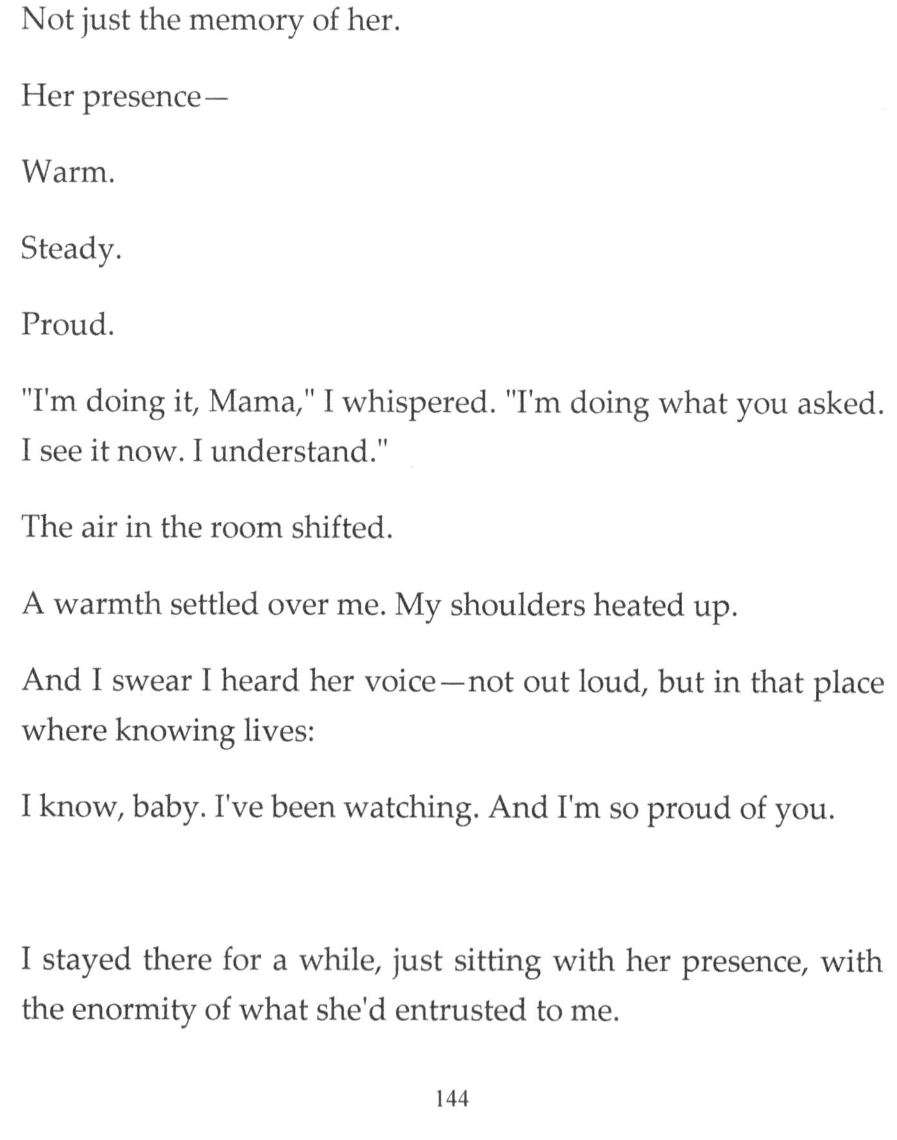

I sat there on the floor, crying, holding her picture, and I felt her.

Not just the memory of her.

Her presence—

Warm.

Steady.

Proud.

"I'm doing it, Mama," I whispered. "I'm doing what you asked. I see it now. I understand."

The air in the room shifted.

A warmth settled over me. My shoulders heated up.

And I swear I heard her voice—not out loud, but in that place where knowing lives:

I know, baby. I've been watching. And I'm so proud of you.

I stayed there for a while, just sitting with her presence, with the enormity of what she'd entrusted to me.

And then I stood up, carefully placed the photo on my altar, and lit a candle beside it.

White. For clarity and guidance.

"Thank you," I said aloud. "Thank you for seeing me. For choosing me. For starting this work so I could finish it."

I pulled a card from my ancestor oracle deck.

What do my ancestors want me to know right now?

The card I turned over was:

"We are with you."

I set it beside my grandmother's photo and smiled through my tears.

That night, I had another dream.

Not a past life this time.

Just my grandmother.

She was in her kitchen again, sitting at the table, a cup of coffee in front of her.

I sat down across from her.

"You knew," I said.

She nodded. "I knew."

"Why didn't you tell me?"

"Because you weren't ready yet," she said simply. "You had to see it for yourself. You had to understand the scope of it. If I'd told you too early, you would've run."

I smiled, because she was right.

"But now you're ready," she continued. "You've seen the pattern. You've felt the pain. You've carried it long enough. And now it's time to end it."

"How?" I asked.

She reached across the table and took my hand.

"You already know," she said. "You've been preparing for this your whole life. You just didn't know it."

She squeezed my hand.

"Go back one more time," she said. "Find the source. The original wound. The moment the curse latched onto our line. And when you find it—cut it loose. Set us all free."

"I'm scared," I admitted.

"I know," she said. "But you're not doing it alone. I'm with you. The ancestors are with you. And you're stronger than you know."

She smiled—that same soft, knowing smile from the photo.

"You're ready, baby. It's time."

I woke up with a clarity I'd never felt before.

No fear.

No doubt.

Just certainty.

I went to my kitchen.

Cooked a big breakfast.

Grits.

Bacon.

Scrambled eggs with cheese.

Coffee.

Afterwards, I went to my altar.

My grandmother's photo was still there, the white candle burned halfway down.

I took a deep breath in.

Exhaled.

And I spoke aloud, to her, to the ancestors, to the part of myself that was finally ready to finish this:

"I'm going to do what you asked. I'm going to take care of the family. Not by keeping everyone together. But by setting us free."

I paused.

"I'm going to find the source. I'm going to see the original wound. And I'm going to put a stop to this. For you. For me. For my descendants. For all the daughters who come after."

The candles flickered.

And I felt it again—that warmth, that presence, that unmistakable sense of being held by something way bigger than myself.

The ancestors.

My grandmother.

And I whispered:

"I got you Mama. I won't let you down."

CHAPTER 12
The First Cut

I walked past my altar, honoring what had taken place in my dream.

The white candles were still burning beside my grandmother's photo, casting soft shadows across the cowrie shells and crystals I'd arranged so carefully over the years.

I felt different.

Not heavy, like I had after the past life sessions.

But clear.

Like something had finally clicked into place.

My eyes drifted to the box of photos still sitting on my bedroom floor.

And underneath it—

My Bible.

The one my grandmother had given me when I was twelve.

The one I hadn't opened in years.

I picked it up, feeling the weight of it in my hands—worn leather, pages soft and thin from decades of use before it came to me.

I didn't know why I was reaching for it.

But my hands knew before my mind did.

I brought it back to my couch and sat down, cross-legged, the Bible in my lap.

"Show me," I whispered. "Show me what I need to see."

I let the book fall open.

Genesis: Chapter 3

Genesis, of course—the beginning.

I stared at the page for a moment, and then I started reading.

Not the way I'd been taught to read it—as a story about sin and punishment and a woman who ruined everything.

But with *new* eyes.

Eyes that had seen past lives, felt generational wounds, watched patterns repeat across centuries.

I read slowly, letting each verse settle.

And when I got to verse 15, I stopped.

"And I will put enmity between thee and the woman, and between thy seed and her seed…"

I read it again.

And again.

And suddenly, I saw it.

"I will put enmity."

Not "there is enmity."

Not "enmity exists."

I will PUT.

Installed.

Programmed.

Inserted into a relationship that was once whole.

I got a check in my spirit. A download was happening.

I grabbed my journal and started writing, my hand moving faster than my thoughts could keep up.

This is it.

This is the SOURCE—the origin.

Not 3,000 years ago.

Not an earthbound soul or entity from one lifetime.

But, the FIRST CUT.

The original fracture—the opposing force.

The moment enmity was installed between woman and woman, mother and daughter, wisdom and compliance.

I kept reading, unpacking the text the way my grandmother had taught me—not literally, but esoterically. Looking for what was underneath the surface.

"And I will put enmity between thee and the woman..."

The serpent is being addressed first.

The serpent—wisdom, embodied knowing, direct access to truth.

And what happens to it?

It's demoted.

"On your belly you shall go, and dust you shall eat."

Pushed down. Grounded. Made low. Earthbound in the most humiliating sense.

Wisdom is no longer upright, luminous, cosmic.

It's something to be stepped on.

Something dangerous.

Something to fear.

"I will put enmity between you and the woman, and between your offspring and her offspring."

This is where the wound becomes generational. Right here.

Before this moment:

- ✓ The woman listens to wisdom
- ✓ Wisdom speaks without fear
- ✓ The body and knowing are aligned

After this moment:

- ✓ Wisdom becomes suspect
- ✓ The woman is taught to fear what she once trusted
- ✓ Inner knowing is reframed as threat

And it doesn't stop with one generation.

It's seeded into time.

Into bloodlines.

Into the very fabric of how mothers and daughters relate to each other.

I kept writing, the words pouring out:

This is not natural hostility.

This is psychological warfare.

This is the installation of a relational distortion that becomes normalized over time.

Mothers are severed from their knowing.

Daughters are punished for theirs.

And the conflict is blamed on THEM—on women—instead of on the system that was built to restrain them.

"Unto the woman he said, I will greatly multiply thy sorrow and thy conception; in sorrow thou shalt bring forth children..."

I paused on this line.

Childbearing.

The Womb—life.

The portal.

Raw feminine energy.

Not just physical birth—

Creation—ideas, art, futures, identities, nations.

Pain is attached to bringing forth anything *new*.

Creation becomes suffering instead of joy.

That's not biology.

That's a leash.

"And thy desire shall be to thy husband, and he shall rule over thee."

This is the reorientation.

The woman is turned away from:

- ✓ Her body
- ✓ Her knowing
- ✓ Her direct relationship with wisdom and turned toward external validation and protection.

Dependence is installed where sovereignty once lived.

What was once partnership becomes dominance.

What was once mutuality becomes command.

What was once listening becomes obedience.

And this is said AFTER the woman has awakened.

So awareness is not celebrated.

It is contained.

I sat back, staring at what I'd written.

And it dawned on me:

This isn't a fall from grace.

This is patriarchy mythologizing itself as divine order.

Wisdom is demoted.

The feminine is disciplined.

The body is punished.

Authority is centralized.

And the deepest trick of all?

The woman is blamed for the system that was built to restrain her.

I paused, pen hovering over the page.

And then I wrote:

This wound didn't just fracture the bond between mother and daughter.

It fractured relationship itself.

What severed women from their knowing also narrowed the emotional lives of men.

Because when women are punished for embodied wisdom, men are raised to enforce that punishment.

When mothers are severed from their power, sons inherit the script of dominance instead of presence.

When daughters are taught that their knowing is dangerous,

sons are taught that vulnerability is weakness.

Healing the Mother Wound does not emasculate men.

It liberates them.

Because when women are no longer punished for knowing, men are no longer required to enforce ignorance.

When women reclaim embodied wisdom, men are no longer stuck performing dominance instead of partnership.

When the enmity is broken, everyone breathes easier.

This is not about blame.

It's about repair.

I set the pen down, tears in my eyes.

Slinging snot.

Because I'd seen it.

In my own family.

In my friend's families.

In my client's families.

The way my male cousins struggled to connect emotionally.

The way they'd been taught that being "strong" meant being silent.

The way they carried their own wounds—different from mine, but rooted in the same fracture.

Genesis 3:15 didn't just curse the women.

It cursed the entire lineage.

No one walked out of that garden whole.

And then I realized, breaking it doesn't just free the daughters—

It frees the sons too.

I thought about my mother.

I didn't inherit her cruelty; I inherited a system—ENMITY—the maternal succession override—designed to stop daughters from finishing what mothers were never allowed to become.

And for the first time, I saw her differently.

Not as a villain.

Not as evil.

But as unintegrated.

I started writing again, faster now:

My mother didn't wake up and decide to wound me.

She was raised inside a woman—her mother—who had already absorbed:

- ✓ Fear of feminine power

- ✓ Punishment for intuition
- ✓ Survival through compliance
- ✓ Love interlaced with control

So by the time she became a mother, the wound was no longer visible to her.

It felt like truth.

That's how curses survive.

They stop feeling like curses.

Like patterns.

I thought about all the times my mother had reacted to me with coldness, with envy, with dismissal, with jealousy and rage that seemed out of proportion to whatever I'd said or done. I thought about the times when I asked about my absent father. It was always a smoldering silence.

And I realized:

I am the serpent in her nervous system.

Not evil.

Not manipulative.

But awakened.

I carried:

- ✓ Insight she never had permission to claim

- ✓ Awareness she was punished for even sensing
- ✓ Questions she learned were dangerous

So, my very presence activated her unresolved fracture.

That doesn't make her malicious.

It makes her unintegrated.

And an unintegrated mother often experiences her daughter's clarity as:

- ✓ Disrespect
- ✓ Rebellion
- ✓ Threat
- ✓ "Thinking she's better"

Because the daughter's knowing touches the mother's loss.

I wrote:

To a wounded mother, a conscious daughter doesn't feel like a child.

She feels like:

- ✓ Exposure
- ✓ Judgment
- ✓ Memory returning

So the mother does what the system taught her to do:

- ✓ Diminish

- ✓ Control
- ✓ Silence
- ✓ Project

Not because she simply despises her daughter—

But because she was never taught how to recognize wisdom when it rises in her own bloodline.

I set my pen down.

A wave of emotion overtook me.

And I cried—the kind of crying that only comes when something very old and very buried finally breaks the surface.

Not the way I'd cried after the past life sessions—raw, broken, drowning in old pain.

This was different.

This was grief for something bigger than me.

Grief for my mother, who inherited a wound she was never given language for.

Grief for her mother, and her mother's mother, and all the women before them who were severed from their own knowing and taught to fear it in their daughters.

Grief for the sons who were taught that strength meant silence, that dominance was manhood, that vulnerability was weakness.

Grief for Eve—the archetypal mother—blamed for seeking

wisdom, punished for awakening, and then used as the justification for every act of control and domination that came after.

I looked at Genesis 3:15 again.

And I saw it—plain as day:

This is the Mother Wound.

Not metaphorical.

Not symbolic.

Literal.

A relational distortion, installed at the level of consciousness, passed down through conditioning, nervous systems, and unspoken rules about what women are allowed to know, to feel, and to be.

My mother carries it.

Her mother was exposed to it.

And every woman before her.

Not because they were weak.

Not because they were evil.

But because the enmity was put there.

Installed.

Seeded into the bloodline.

And normalized over millennia until it felt like truth.

I stood up and went to my altar.

Lit another candle for solace and clarity.

And I spoke aloud, to my grandmother, to the ancestors, to every mother and daughter in my line:

"I see it now. The first cut. The original fracture. The moment enmity was inserted between mothers and daughters.

"This is the root.

"But it ends with me.

"Not because I hate her.

"Not because I'm stronger or better or more enlightened.

"But because I refuse to pass it forward.

"I am breaking the curse. I am severing the cord. I am choosing integration over inheritance."

I pulled a card from my oracle deck.

Adrenaline flooded my system.

The card I turned over read:

"You are the last generation to carry it."

I set it on the altar beside my grandmother's photo.

And I whispered:

"I'm ready."

Pam's intuition was right. I didn't need to go back to another past life.

There wasn't an entity attachment from hundreds of years ago.

The source wasn't one woman in one lifetime.

The source was Genesis 3:15.

The archetypal wound.

The original severance.

The installation of enmity between woman and wisdom, mother and daughter, knowing and compliance.

And the cure wasn't exorcism.

It was integration.

Reclaiming the knowing my mother was taught to fear.

Reclaiming the wisdom my lineage was severed from.

Reclaiming the direct relationship with truth that patriarchy tried to eradicate.

And then sealing it through ritual.

I looked at the calendar.

I needed time to prepare.

Time to gather what I needed.

Time to call in the ancestors properly.

But I knew—with a certainty that felt like my grandmother's hand on my shoulder—that the ritual was coming.

The final severance.

The curse-breaking.

The moment I would light the candles, speak the prayers, and watch as the confirmation came.

All of it telling me the same thing:

You did it. The line is free. The wound is finally healed. The curse is over.

I bookmarked the page with the attached red ribbon and closed the Bible.

And I made a promise—to my grandmother, to the ancestors, and to myself:

"I will do this. I will break the curse. Not just for me. But for every daughter who comes after. For every mother who never got the chance to heal. For every woman severed from her own knowing. For every son who was taught that was strength.

"Genesis 3:15 installed the enmity.

"But I am removing it.

"The first cut happened in the garden.

"But the final cut happens here.

"With me.

"Now."

CHAPTER 13
Point of No Return

I didn't rush into the ritual.

I couldn't.

This wasn't something you did on impulse, half-prepared, with whatever happened to be lying around.

This was the culmination of everything—every past life session, every moment of grief, every card pulled, every prayer whispered, every tear cried.

Break the curse.

Free the bloodline.

And I needed to do it right.

I gave myself two weeks.

Two weeks to prepare my space, my body, my spirit.

Two weeks to gather what I needed.

Two weeks to sit with the enormity of what I was about to do.

Two weeks until the last full moon of the year. A supermoon.

Week One: Gathering

I started with a list.

Not just of materials, but of intentions:

- ✓ What was I calling in?
- ✓ What was I banishing?
- ✓ What did I want the ancestors to witness?
- ✓ I sat at my altar with my journal and wrote:
- ✓ I am breaking the Genesis 3:15 curse.
- ✓ I am severing the enmity installed between mothers and daughters.
- ✓ I am reclaiming the knowing my lineage was severed from.
- ✓ I am freeing every woman in my line—past, present, and future—from the wound that learned to behave like a living thing.
- ✓ I am the last generation to carry this.

I read it aloud.

And I felt the ancestors lean in.

I needed candles.

Specific ones.

Not just any candles from the grocery store.

I went to the botanica—the small shop on the edge of town that smelled like herbs and prayers and had been run by the same family for three generations.

The woman behind the counter looked up when I walked in.

"You're doing big work," she said. Not a question. A statement.

I nodded.

"I need candles. Red. Black. White."

She didn't ask why.

She just nodded and went to the back room.

When she returned, she placed chime candles on the counter.

"For the work you're doing," she said, "you'll want to dress them. Anoint them. Speak your intention into them before you light them."

"What oil?" I asked.

She reached under the counter and pulled out a small bottle.

"Uncrossing oil," she said. "For breaking curses, cutting cords, severing what shouldn't be attached. And this—" She placed another bottle beside it. "Protection oil. For sealing what you've broken."

I bought both.

I needed ancestor money.

The kind with gold foil, printed with blessings in languages I didn't fully understand but felt in my bones.

I bought a thick stack.

Enough to honor every woman in my line who had carried the wound and never got the chance to break it.

I needed something to represent the bloodline.

Something physical.

Something I could hold, speak to, release.

I thought about using a piece of red thread—traditional, symbolic.

But then I remembered:

The photo taken at my wedding reception.

My grandmother wearing her shawl. Sitting in her wheelchair.

My mother standing behind her in the shadows.

I pulled it from the wedding photo album stored in the closet.

I looked into my grandmother's eyes.

"I'm doing this for you, Mama," I whispered. "For all of us."

Week Two: Cleansing

The week before the ritual, I cleansed everything.

My apartment. My body. My spirit.

I started with my space.

Burned sage in every room, letting the smoke curl into corners, clearing out stagnant energy, anything that didn't belong.

I washed the floors and walls with saltwater and Florida water.

I opened every window and let fresh air move through.

I cleaned my altar—carefully, reverently—removing all my spiritual tools, wiping down the surface, and then rebuilding it with intention.

On the left: my wedding reception photo of my grandmother and mother.

In the center: A wooden square. The three candles (red, black, white).

To the right: the ancestor money, neatly stacked.

In front: my grandmother's cowrie shells, my tarot deck, my ancestor oracle deck, a small glass of water, some twine for tying the candles, and the oils.

I cleansed my body.

Took a spiritual bath—Sea salt, rosemary, lavender, dragon's blood, a few drops of uncrossing oil.

I sat in the water and prayed.

To the Most High. To my grandmother. To the ancestors. To the part of me that was ready to let go.

"I release what is not mine to carry," I said aloud, my voice echoing in the small bathroom. "I release the wound. I release the enmity. I release the program."

I thanked the Most High and my spiritual team for helping me.

I stayed in the water until it went cold.

I fasted.

Not from all food—I'm not built for that.

But from noise.

No TV. No social media. No music that wasn't intentional.

I wanted to be quiet enough to hear the ancestors when they spoke.

I wanted to be still enough to feel the shift when it happened.

The Night Before

The night before the ritual, I couldn't sleep.

Not from anxiety—

From anticipation.

I lay in bed, staring at the ceiling, feeling the weight of what was coming.

And I asked myself:

Am I ready?

The answer came immediately.

Not in words.

But in a warmth that spread through my chest.

Yes.

I got up and went to my altar.

Lit a white candle—just a small one, for clarity.

I burned the ancestor money.

And I pulled one card from my ancestor oracle deck.

What do I need to know before the ritual?

The card I turned over read:

"We are with you."

I pulled a tarot card.

Strength.

I'm the woman in white standing beside the lion that has been roaring through my lineage.

The Divine Feminine in her highest form.

I set both cards beside my grandmother's photo and smiled.

"I know," I whispered. "I feel you."

It's Time

The clock showed 9 p.m.

I didn't rush.

I sat at my kitchen table in silence for a few minutes.

The bright silver light of the supermoon streamed through my kitchen window and charged something in me I hadn't known was depleted.

And then I went to my altar and began.

I prepared the candles first.

The red one for life, blood, the maternal line, the fire that burns through what no longer serves.

I carved my mother's name on it.

The black one for protection, banishment, the void, death and rebirth.

I tied the red and black candles together with twine.

I carved my name on the white candle.

I anointed each one with uncrossing oil, rubbing it from the base to the wick, speaking my intention as I worked:

"This candle represents the breaking of the curse. The severing of the Genesis 3:15 curse. The end of enmity between mothers and daughters in my line."

I did this for all three candles.

I arrange them on the wooden board on my altar in a triangle—symbol of ascension and sovereignty:

Red. Black. The triangle base.

The old energy and the transforming energy sit beneath me.

White. The triangle point. I set it on a thick wooden coaster so it would he higher than the red and black candles.

I'm standing in my authority. My sovereignty.

I placed the water glass near the cards.

I stood my wedding reception picture up on a small easel.

I lit incense—frankincense and myrrh, the scents of ritual, reverence, and protection.

And then I sat.

Quiet.

Still.

Waiting for the ancestors to tell me it was time.

I called the daughters. The mothers.

I felt them gather.

Not just my grandmother.

But others.

The women who came before her.

The mothers and daughters who carried the wound and never got to break it.

I felt them standing behind me, around me, filling the room with a presence so thick I could barely breathe.

And I heard my grandmother's voice—not out loud, but clear as day:

"It's time, baby. Do the work."

The room shifted.

Not dramatically.

Subtly.

Like something had decided to stay.

The air grew thick. Crowded with unfinished stories.

With words swallowed whole with grief that never got a name.

With love that learned how to survive by hardening.

I could feel where their lives stopped short.

Where endurance replaced choice.

Where silence was mistaken for strength.

This wasn't about bravery.

Or belief.

Or faith.

It was about consent.

Mine.

I was no longer agreeing to carry what was never mine to complete.

I took a deep breath—

And decreed:

"I break the curse of enmity between my mother and me—between the mothers and daughters of this bloodline. No more will you stalk us through lifetimes, realms, or dimensions—known and unknown. You will not find us in spirit nor in flesh. Love is the salve that seals the wound. Love is the new inheritance. This curse ends with me for all eternity. So shall it be."

.

CHAPTER 14
The Reckoning

I lit the red candle first. Black candle second. White candle last.

The red candle flame caught immediately—no hesitation, no flicker.

Just pure, hungry fire.

Within seconds, the flame was burning higher than any candle I'd ever seen.

Seven inches.

Eight.

The flame leaping and dancing like it had been waiting for this moment.

Like it knew what it was here to do.

I lit the black candle.

Its flame was different—low, steady, grounded.

It burned slow, deliberate, like it was holding space while the red candle did its wild, consuming work.

Protection.

Banishment.

The void.

Witnessing.

I lit the white candle last.

My name carved into the wax.

The flame caught clean and bright.

Steady.

Elevated on its coaster—it stood higher than the red and black candles.

Sovereign.

Clear.

Mine.

I stepped back, watching.

The red candle—my mother's name carved into the wax—was

consuming itself.

Fast.

Too fast.

The wax melted in rivulets, pooling at the base, but the flame kept climbing, kept reaching, kept burning.

And then I saw it—

The twine.

The cord I'd tied between the red and black candles.

It was starting to smoke.

I held my breath.

The flame from the red candle licked at the twine.

Once.

Twice.

And then—

Snap.

The twine severed.

Fell away.

Burned clean through.

The red candle and the black candle—no longer bound.

I gasped.

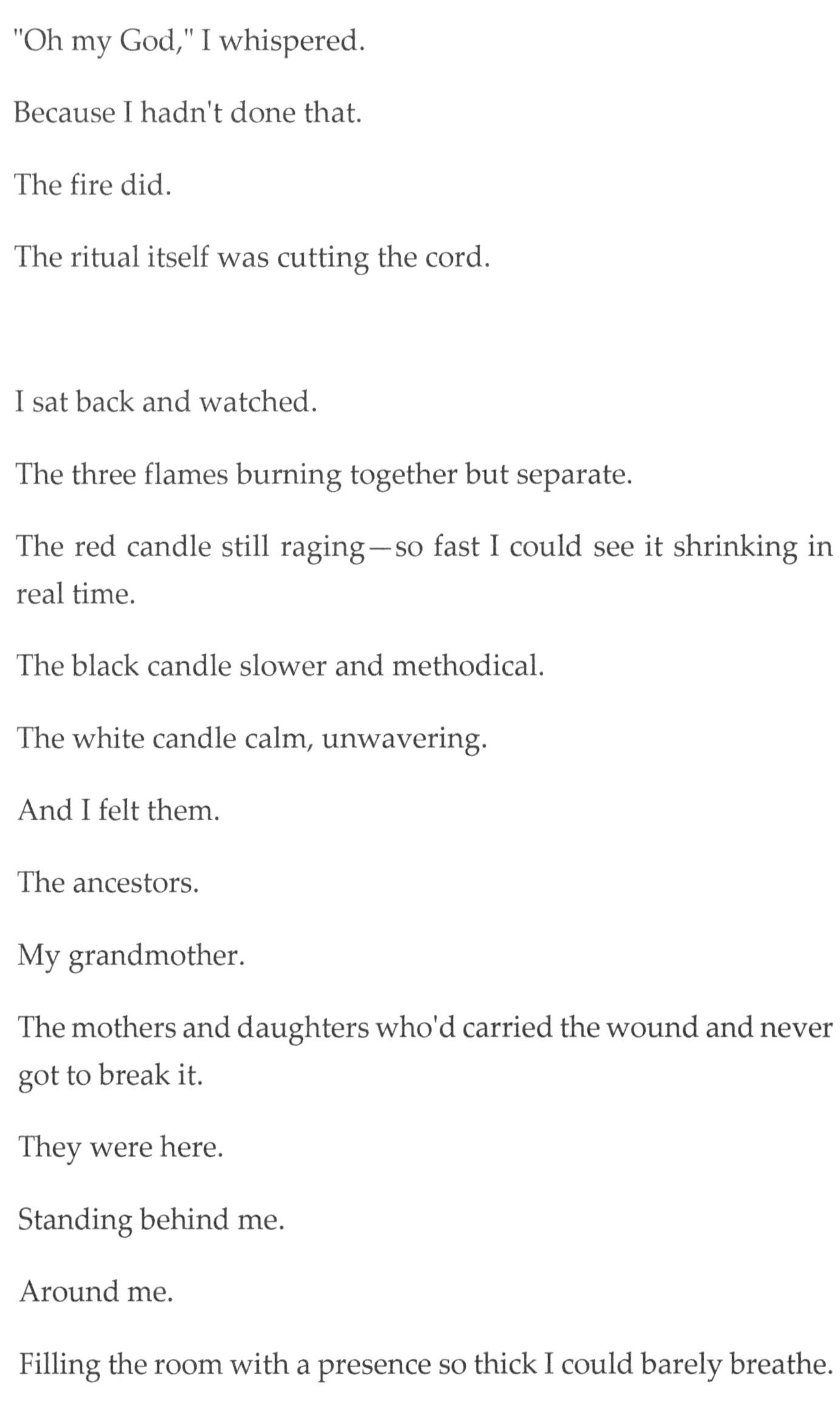

"Oh my God," I whispered.

Because I hadn't done that.

The fire did.

The ritual itself was cutting the cord.

I sat back and watched.

The three flames burning together but separate.

The red candle still raging—so fast I could see it shrinking in real time.

The black candle slower and methodical.

The white candle calm, unwavering.

And I felt them.

The ancestors.

My grandmother.

The mothers and daughters who'd carried the wound and never got to break it.

They were here.

Standing behind me.

Around me.

Filling the room with a presence so thick I could barely breathe.

Again, I spoke aloud, my voice steady:

"I call upon the mothers and daughters of my bloodline. The ones who came before. The ones who will come after. I call upon my grandmother, who started this work. I call upon the ancestors who've been waiting.

"Witness this.

"I am revoking the Genesis 3:15 curse.

"I break the power of enmity spoken over our bloodline.

"I am severing the enmity installed between mothers and daughters.

"I am reclaiming the knowing my lineage was severed from.

"I am freeing every woman in my line—past, present, and future—from the wound that learned to behave like a living thing.

"I am the last generation who will suffer from this."

The red candle burned faster.

The flame leapt higher—so high I thought it might catch the wall on fire.

I watched, transfixed, as the wax melted away, layer after layer, the candle consuming itself in minutes instead of hours.

I grabbed my phone.

I don't know why.

Instinct, maybe.

I needed to capture this.

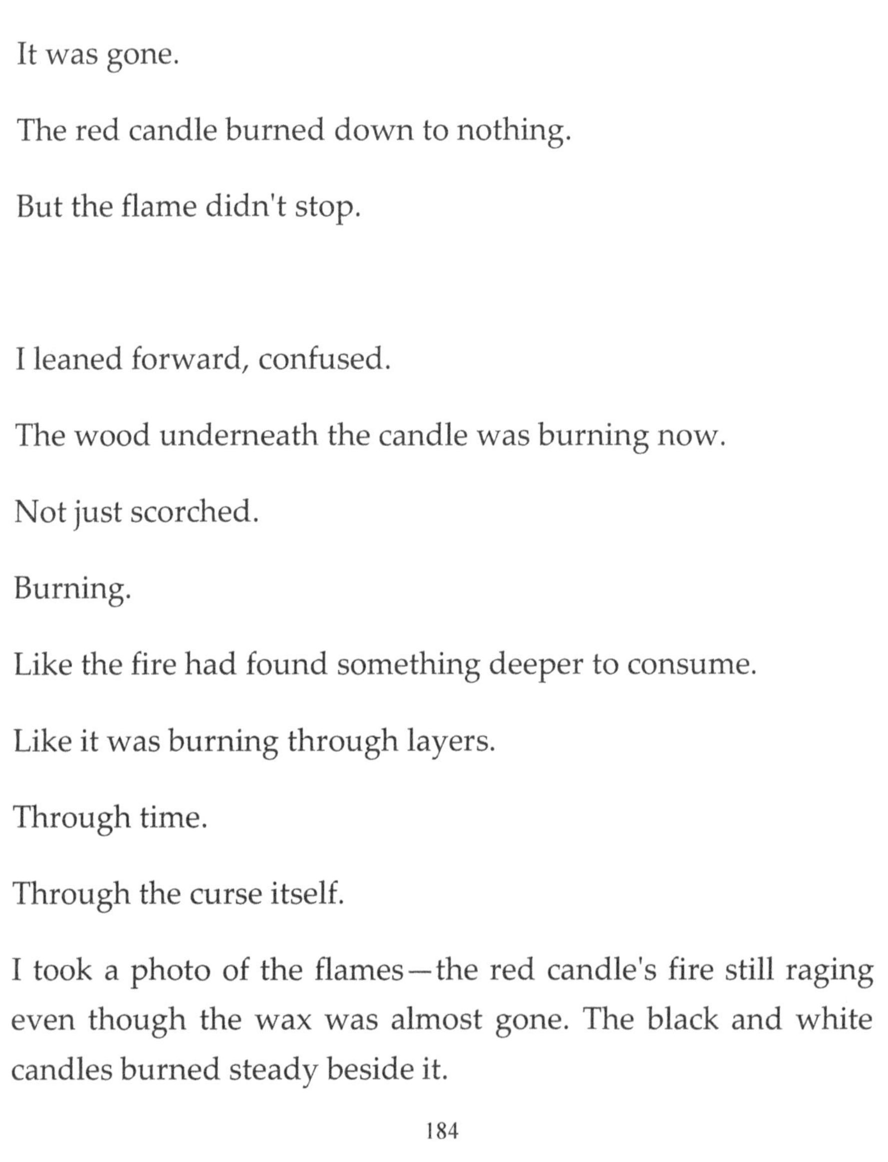

Minutes later—

It was gone.

The red candle burned down to nothing.

But the flame didn't stop.

I leaned forward, confused.

The wood underneath the candle was burning now.

Not just scorched.

Burning.

Like the fire had found something deeper to consume.

Like it was burning through layers.

Through time.

Through the curse itself.

I took a photo of the flames—the red candle's fire still raging even though the wax was almost gone. The black and white candles burned steady beside it.

When I looked at the photo—

I froze.

There, in the center of the flames, clear as day:

A hand.

Not just a hand—

A hand and forearm—maybe six inches past the wrist.

Reaching up.

And around it, unmistakable:

A charred broken chain.

I stared at the photo, my heart pounding.

The ancestors were showing me.

The chain is broken off the bloodline.

The hand is reaching toward freedom.

It's done.

The wood kept burning.

Ten minutes.

Twenty.

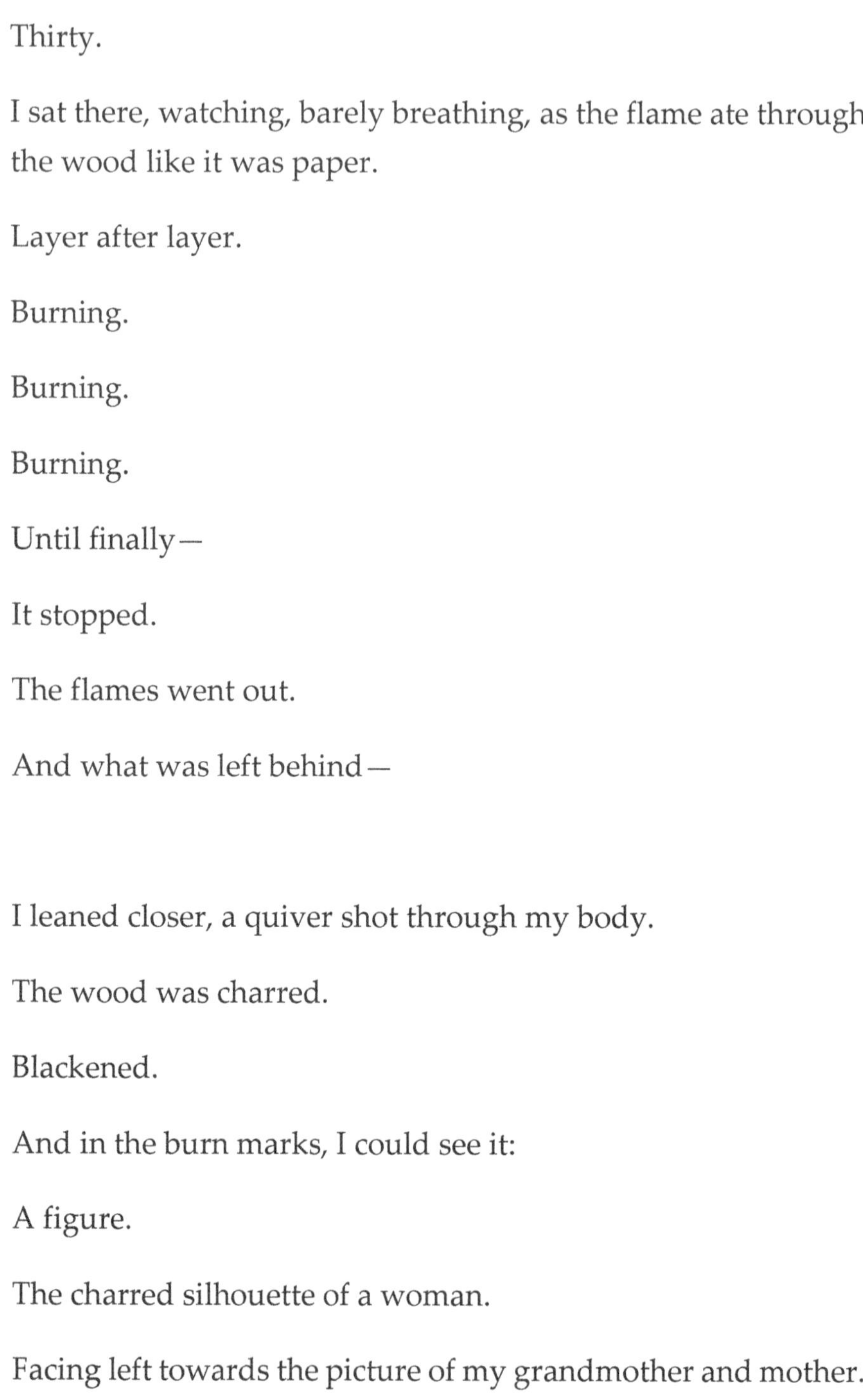

Thirty.

I sat there, watching, barely breathing, as the flame ate through the wood like it was paper.

Layer after layer.

Burning.

Burning.

Burning.

Until finally—

It stopped.

The flames went out.

And what was left behind—

I leaned closer, a quiver shot through my body.

The wood was charred.

Blackened.

And in the burn marks, I could see it:

A figure.

The charred silhouette of a woman.

Facing left towards the picture of my grandmother and mother.

Her blackened outline unmistakable—head, shoulders, hair,

face, torso.

She was looking back.

Toward the past.

Toward the mothers and daughters who came before.

But she wasn't moving forward anymore.

She was released.

Seen.

Witnessed.

Free.

I sat back, tears streaming down my face.

"I see you," I whispered. "I see you, and you're free now. We're all free."

The black candle was on its last flicker.

Moments later—

It went out.

And as I watched, the wax began to pool at the base.

Not just pooling.

Forming.

I tilted my head, trying to see it clearly.

And then I realized—

The wax had formed the shape of a baby.

Curled.

Tiny.

Perfect.

Like a child in the womb.

I covered my mouth with my hand, sobbing now.

The future daughters.

Protected.

Safe.

Born free.

The black candle—protection, death and rebirth—had covered them.

Had sealed them.

The curse was broken.

And the daughters who would come after were already being held.

The white candle burned steady.

Calm.

Unwavering.

My candle.

My sovereignty.

Standing above the old energy.

Elevated.

Clear.

Free.

When the white candle finally burned out, I sat quietly for what seemed like an eternity. Staring at the wood.

The room felt different.

Lighter.

Open.

Like something that had been pressing down on me my entire life had finally lifted.

But then—

A fleeting thought.

Small.

Quiet.

Familiar.

Did it work?

Did it really work, or am I just telling myself it did?

I looked at my altar.

The charred wood with the woman's image.

The black wax shaped like a baby.

I looked at the photo on my phone showing the hand reaching up in the flames, the broken chain.

And I knew I needed one more confirmation.

I reached for my ancestor oracle deck.

Shuffled.

Pulled one card.

"We Crown You for Your Work."

I pulled a tarot card.

The Three of Cups.

Three women.

Dancing.

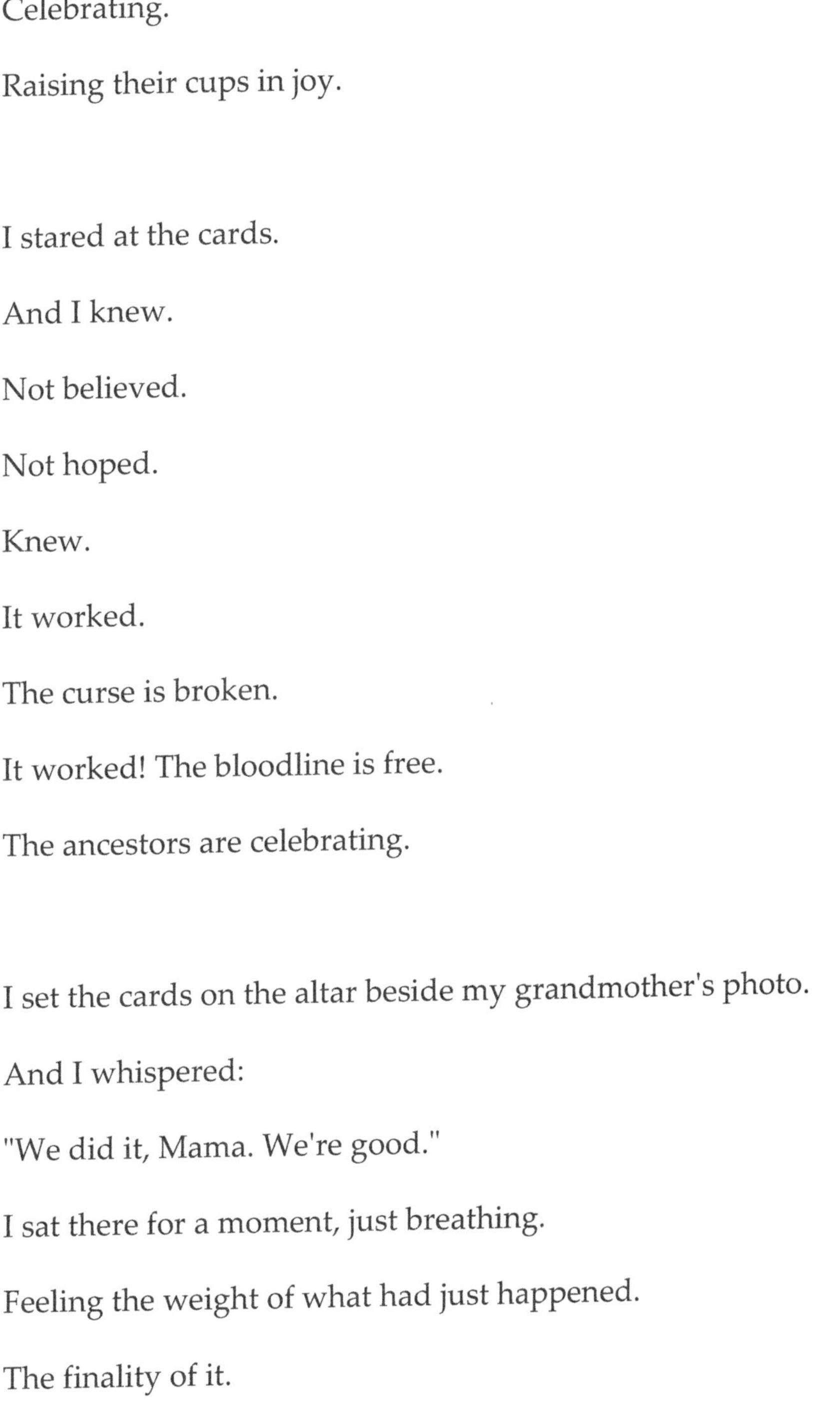

Celebrating.

Raising their cups in joy.

I stared at the cards.

And I knew.

Not believed.

Not hoped.

Knew.

It worked.

The curse is broken.

It worked! The bloodline is free.

The ancestors are celebrating.

I set the cards on the altar beside my grandmother's photo.

And I whispered:

"We did it, Mama. We're good."

I sat there for a moment, just breathing.

Feeling the weight of what had just happened.

The finality of it.

The completion.

And for the first time in my life, I felt something I'd never felt before:

Peace.

Not the absence of conflict.

But the presence of wholeness.

The knowing that I didn't have to carry this anymore.

That the daughters who came after me wouldn't have to carry it either.

That the wound—the one that had been passed down for millennia, the one installed in Genesis 3:15—

Stopped here.

With me.

I pulled out my journal and wrote:

Tonight, under the supermoon, I broke the curse.

The red candle burned fast and severed the twine itself.

The wood underneath kept burning, and the ancestor's image appeared in the charred wood—the woman who carried the first wound, now released.

The black candle's wax formed a baby—the future daughters,

protected and free.

The white candle burned steady—me, standing in my power—in my sovereignty.

I took a photo of the flames and saw a hand reaching up, a charred, broken chain beside it.

I pulled the Three of Cups.

The ancestors are celebrating.

It's done.

The Genesis 3:15 program is severed.

The enmity between mothers and daughters is broken off this bloodline.

I am free.

We are all free.

I closed the journal.

Looked at the altar one more time.

The charred image in the wood.

The baby in the wax.

My grandmother's photo.

The Three of Cups and my oracle card.

And I smiled.

Not a relieved smile.

A victorious smile.

Because I had done what I came here to do.

I had broken what my grandmother couldn't.

I had freed what the ancestors had been waiting for someone to free.

I had taken the wound that learned to behave like a living thing—

And starved it to death.

CHAPTER 15
After the Fire

I woke up the next morning feeling…strange.

Not bad strange.

Just different.

Like I'd gone to sleep as one person and woke up as someone else.

I lay in bed for a while, staring at the ceiling, trying to identify what had shifted.

And then I realized:

The heaviness was gone.

The weight I'd been carrying my entire life—the one that sat on my chest every morning, the one that made even breathing feel like work—gone.

I got up and brushed my teeth.

Checked my altar.

Everything was still there, exactly as I'd left it the night before.

The charred wood with the ancestor's image burned into it.

The black wax shaped like a baby.

The wedding photo of my grandmother and mother.

The Three of Cups and the We Crown You cards.

I picked up the wood carefully, turning it in my hands.

The woman's image was so clear.

Facing left.

Looking back.

But not moving forward anymore.

Released.

I reached for my phone and zoomed in on the image of the ancestor and took a photo of it.

Then I took a close-up photo of the baby in the wax.

I sent them both to Pam with a simple message:

"It's done."

She responded immediately:

"I can feel it. Well done. Call me when you're ready to process."

I made coffee.

Grabbed a blueberry muffin.

Sat at my kitchen table…and I waited.

Waited for the doubt to creep back in.

Waited for the fear.

Waited for the voice that would tell me I'd imagined it all, that nothing had really changed.

But it didn't come.

Instead, I just felt…clear.

Like I'd been looking through a foggy window my entire life and someone had finally wiped it clean…

Week One

The first week after the ritual, I was gentle with myself.

I didn't push.

Didn't try to "get back to normal."

I rested.

I drank plenty of water.

I journaled.

Spent time at my altar, talking to my grandmother, thanking the ancestors.

And I watched.

Watched for signs that the curse-breaking had worked.

Watched for any residual energy trying to creep back in.

Watched for my mother.

She was quiet.

No calls. No texts. No attempts to reach out.

At first, I thought maybe it was just coincidence.

But then I remembered what Pam had said months ago:

"When you cut a cord, sometimes the other person doesn't even know it happened consciously. But their energy knows. And they'll either respect the boundary—or they'll panic and try harder to get back in."

I braced myself for the panic.

For the escalation.

For the extinction burst.

Week Two

It came on a Tuesday.

A text.

Not from my mother directly—she knew I'd blocked her.

But from one of my brothers.

Subject line: *Your mother wants to talk to you.*

I stared at it for a long moment before opening it.

The message was short:

"Hey, I know you and mom have your issues, but she asked me to reach out. She says she's been trying to get in touch with you and you're not responding. She's really hurt. She just wants to talk. Can you at least give her a call?"

I read it twice.

And I felt…nothing.

Not anger.

Not guilt.

Not the old pull to explain myself, to justify my boundaries, to make someone else understand.

Just nothing.

I deleted the text without responding.

And I pulled a card.

What do I need to know about this?

Eight of Swords, reversed.

The woman who was once bound and blindfolded—

Now free.

The swords that once trapped her—

Fallen away.

She can see clearly now.

She can walk away.

I set the card down and smiled.

"Nice try," I whispered. "But I'm not going back."

Week Three

Another attempt.

This time, a text from a cousin.

"I ran into your mom today. She's really going through it. I think she misses you. Maybe you should reach out?"

I chose not to respond and deleted it.

And then, two days later—an email.

This time from my mother's sister—my aunt.

"I don't know what happened between you two, but your mother is my sister and I hate seeing her so upset. She says you won't talk to her. Whatever she did, don't you think it's time to forgive? Life's too short to hold grudges."

I read the email slowly.

And I noticed something:

It didn't land the way it used to.

Before the ritual, an email like this would have sent me spiraling.

Would have made me question myself.

Am I being too harsh? Am I holding a grudge? Should I just try one more time?

But now?

Now I could see it clearly:

This isn't about me.

This is about her discomfort.

And her discomfort is not my responsibility.

I wrote back—calm, clear, brief:

"Auntie, I appreciate your concern, but my relationship with my mother is between me and her. I've made the decision that's healthiest for me, and I'm at peace with it. I'm not asking anyone to take sides or get involved. I hope you can respect that."

I hit send.

And I felt powerful.

Not defensive.

Not guilty.

Powerful.

Week Four

The attempts slowed.

One more text from a cousin.

One more email from a family friend who "just wanted to check in."

Each time, I either ignored it or responded with the same calm boundary:

"This is between me and my mother. I'm at peace with my decision. Please respect that."

And each time, I felt stronger.

More certain.

I called Pam.

"She's trying," I told her. "She's using other people to get to me. But it's not working."

"Good," Pam said. "That's the extinction burst. The ancestral curse you severed is in collapse. It no longer has a bloodline to feed through, so it's thrashing. Trying every doorway it once used. But it can't reach you anymore. The line has been cut."

"But it's not working," I repeated.

"No," Pam said. "Because you're not giving it an opening. You did the work. You cut the cord. And now you're holding the boundary. That's how you know it worked."

I thought about that.

"What if she tries to contact me directly?" I asked. "What if she shows up at my door or something?"

Pam was quiet for a moment.

"Then you hold the line," she said simply. "You don't engage. You don't explain. You don't justify. You just say, 'I'm not available for this conversation,' and you close the door. Literally, if you have to."

"And if she escalates?"

"Then you document it, and you take whatever steps you need to keep yourself safe. But I don't think it'll come to that. From what you've told me, she's not violent—she's manipulative. And manipulation only works if you engage."

I nodded, even though she couldn't see me.

"You're right."

"You've done the hardest part," Pam said. "You broke the curse. You freed the bloodline. Now you just have to live in that freedom. And that means not letting anyone—not your mother, not your family—not anyone—pull you back into the old pattern."

Month Two

The attempts stopped.

Completely.

No more emails. No more texts. No more cousins or aunts or family friends reaching out on her behalf—not even my brothers.

Just…silence.

At first, I waited for the other shoe to drop.

But it never did.

And I realized:

She gave up.

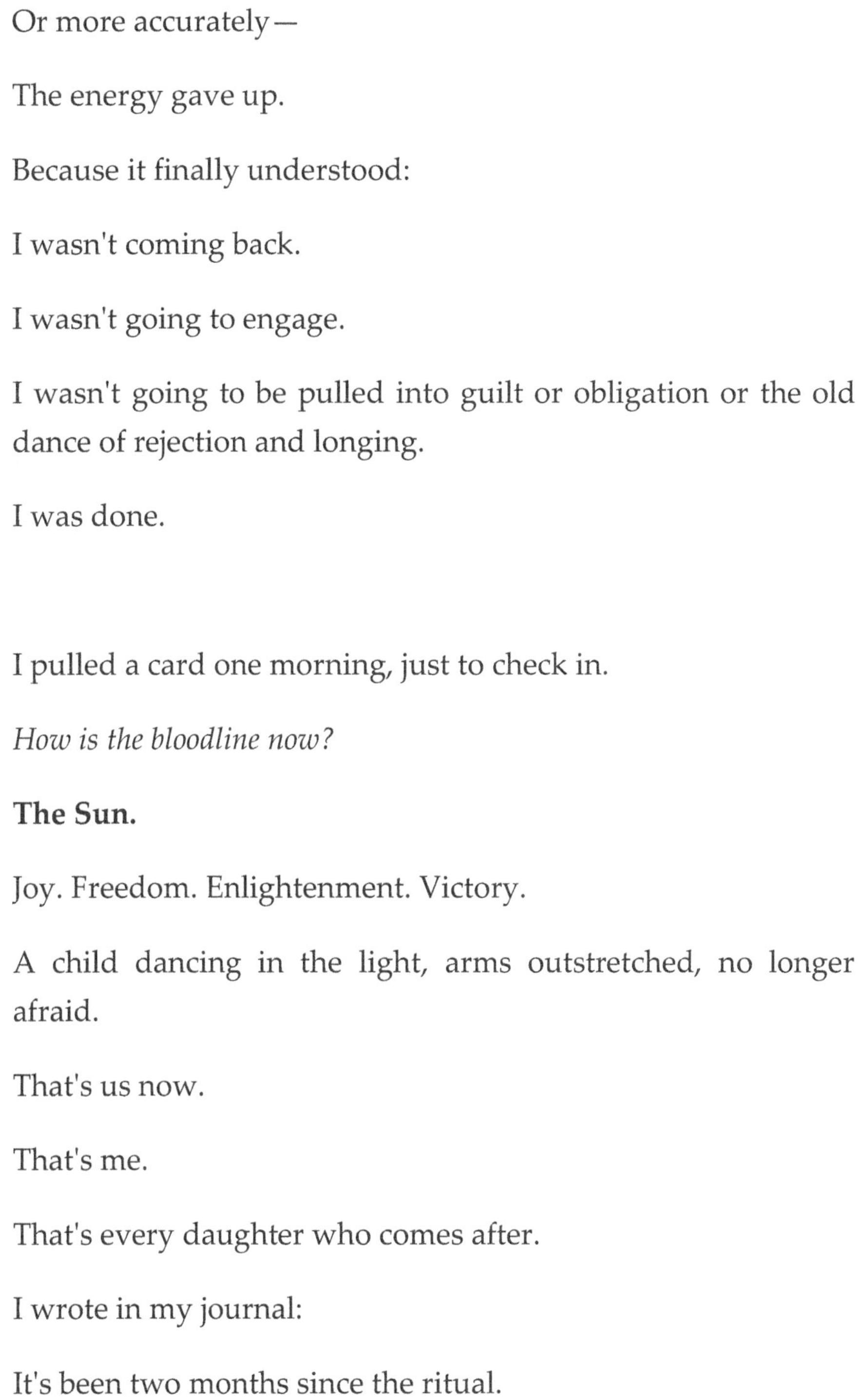

Or more accurately—

The energy gave up.

Because it finally understood:

I wasn't coming back.

I wasn't going to engage.

I wasn't going to be pulled into guilt or obligation or the old dance of rejection and longing.

I was done.

I pulled a card one morning, just to check in.

How is the bloodline now?

The Sun.

Joy. Freedom. Enlightenment. Victory.

A child dancing in the light, arms outstretched, no longer afraid.

That's us now.

That's me.

That's every daughter who comes after.

I wrote in my journal:

It's been two months since the ritual.

My mother tried to reach me through other people, but I held the boundary.

She's quiet now.

And I'm free.

Not just free of her—but free of the curse.

Free of the wound that told me I wasn't enough.

Free of the belief that I had to keep trying, keep hoping, keep waiting for her to love me the way I needed.

I don't need that anymore.

I have my grandmother's love.

I have the ancestors' love.

I have my own love.

And that's enough.

More than enough.

It's everything.

I went to my altar and lit a yellow candle.

For gratitude. For celebration. For victory.

And I spoke aloud:

"Thank you.

"To my grandmother, who started this work and passed me the mantle.

"To the ancestors, who held me through every session, every moment of doubt, every rejection, every tear.

"To the ancient ancestor whose image burned into the wood—you're free now. We're all free.

"To the future daughters—you'll never carry this wound. You'll never know what it feels like to be rejected by the woman who gave you life. You're protected. You're safe. You're loved.

"And to me—

"I did it.

"I broke the curse.

"I freed the bloodline.

"I am the last generation to carry the Mother Wound.

"And I'm so damn proud of myself."

The candle flickered.

And I felt them—

My grandmother.

The ancestors.

The future daughters.

All of them, standing with me.

Celebrating.

I pulled one more card.

Not asking a question this time.

Just…checking in.

Seeing what the ancestors wanted me to know.

The World.

Completion.

Fulfillment.

The end of a cycle.

Victory.

I set the card on the altar and smiled.

"Yeah," I whispered. "We did it."

.

CHAPTER 16
Recoded Legacy

Six months had passed since the ritual.

Six months of living in a freedom I didn't know was possible.

Half a year of waking up without the weight.

Six months of moving through the world as someone who was no longer defined by what her mother couldn't give her.

Six beautiful months of having fun with my friends.

I was different now.

Not in some grand, dramatic way.

But in the small, quiet ways that actually matter.

I didn't flinch when someone mentioned my mother's name.

I didn't spiral when I saw mothers and daughters together in public—the ones who laughed easily, who held hands, who looked at each other with uncomplicated love.

I didn't feel that old, familiar ache of "Why not me?"

Because I know now:

This wasn't just about me.

I didn't realize until much later that what I called anxiety was my nervous system keeping watch.

It learned early on that safety could shift without warning, so it stayed awake for me—quietly, faithfully, for years.

I don't blame it for that anymore. I thank it. And I let it know, lovingly, that the danger it was preparing for has passed.

Healing didn't arrive as peace; it arrived as a refusal to stay on alert.

As the ability to feel my feet on the floor and not scan for exits.

That was when I knew the work had landed—not as an idea, but as a settling in my body.

I sat at my altar on a Saturday morning, the same way I'd done hundreds of times before.

But this time felt different.

This time, I wasn't asking for guidance.

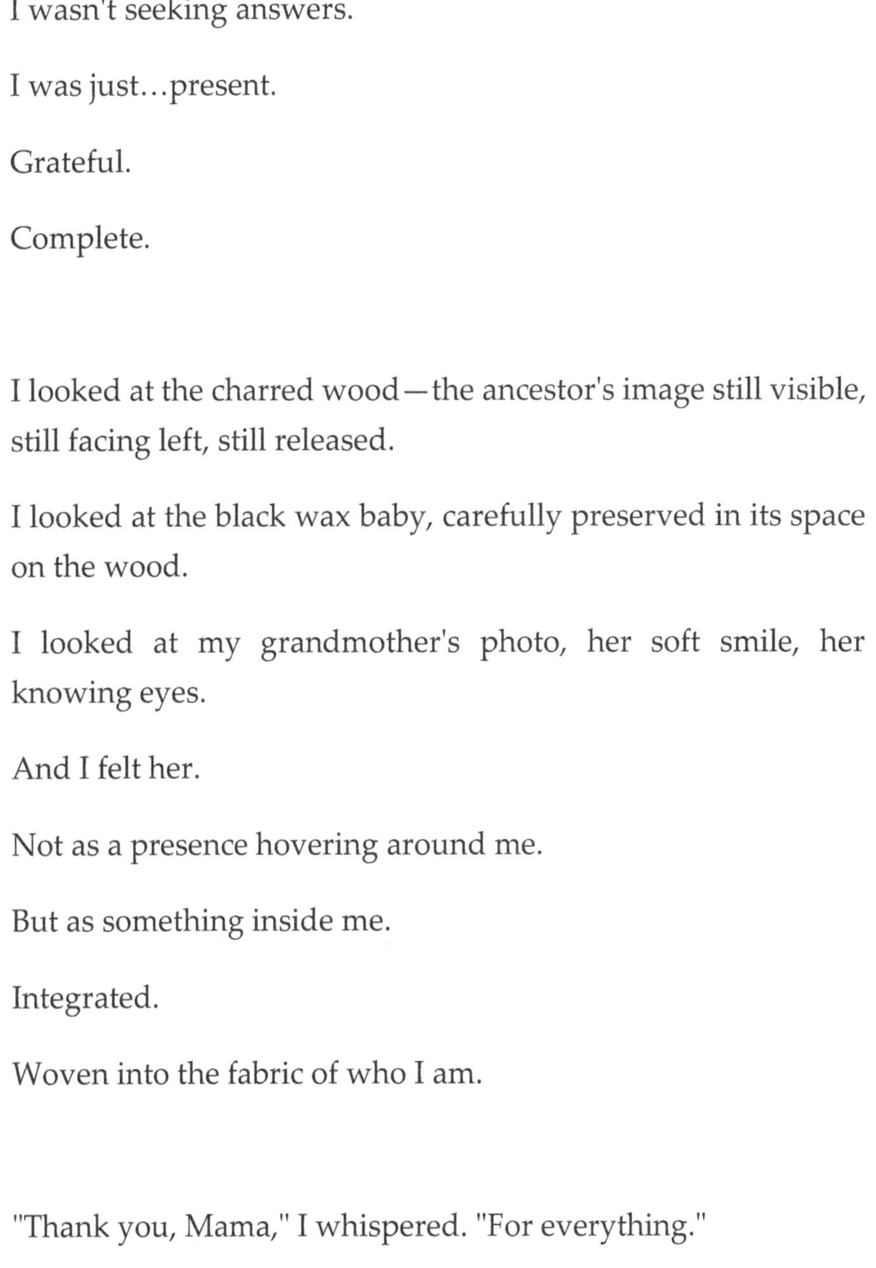

I wasn't seeking answers.

I was just…present.

Grateful.

Complete.

I looked at the charred wood—the ancestor's image still visible, still facing left, still released.

I looked at the black wax baby, carefully preserved in its space on the wood.

I looked at my grandmother's photo, her soft smile, her knowing eyes.

And I felt her.

Not as a presence hovering around me.

But as something inside me.

Integrated.

Woven into the fabric of who I am.

"Thank you, Mama," I whispered. "For everything."

I pulled out my journal.

Not to document pain this time.

But to document freedom. I wrote:

Six months ago, I broke the curse.

I severed the Genesis 3:15 tether.

I freed the bloodline.

And now I know what it feels like to live without the Mother Wound.

It feels like:

- ✓ Breathing all the way down to my toes
- ✓ Trusting my own knowing without second-guessing
- ✓ Setting boundaries without guilt
- ✓ Saying no without explanation
- ✓ Loving myself not in spite of what my mother couldn't give me, but because I finally understand that her inability to love me was never about my worth.

It feels like wholeness.

I paused, pen hovering over the page.

And then I wrote something I'd never written before:

I forgive her.

Not because she asked for it.

Not because she earned it.

Not because I'm "supposed to."

But because holding onto the anger was keeping me bound.

I forgive her for being unable to love me.

I forgive her for carrying a wound she didn't know how to heal.

I forgive her for passing it down.

And I forgive myself—

For all the years I blamed myself—felt sorry for myself.

For all the times I tried to earn love that was never mine to earn.

For all the energy I spent hoping she would change.

For not realizing sooner that division is not the wound—the refusal to see it is.

I forgive us both.

And I set us both free.

I set the pen down, quiet tears rolling down my face.

Not sad tears.

Release tears.

Because I finally get it:

Forgiveness wasn't about condoning what she did.

It wasn't about reconciliation.

It wasn't about pretending that harm didn't happen.

Forgiveness was about releasing the expectation that the past should have been different. It was about accepting what was and choosing freedom anyway.

I pulled a card.

What do the ancestors want me to focus on today?

Temperance.

Balance. Integration. Purpose. Alchemy.

The angel pouring water between two cups, mixing light and dark, past and future, wound and healing.

Not erasure.

Integration.

I smiled.

"Yeah," I whispered. "I get it."

I thought about my mother.

Not with anger anymore.

Not with longing—but with…clarity and truth.

I must keep my distance—without it, mercy becomes access.

She was still out there, living her life, carrying the wound she'd always carried.

She would probably never do the work I did.

I don't expect her too.

She may never understand the gravity of what she lost when she walked away from me.

Sadly, she would probably die with the distortion still intact—carrying it and its toxicity into her next life—

Like a bag lady.

Because I couldn't save her.

I could only save myself.

And by saving myself, I saved the daughters who would come after me.

That was enough.

I stood up and went to the window.

Looked out at the city, the people moving through their lives, carrying their own wounds, their own patterns, their own unfinished business.

And I felt a surge of compassion.

Not just for my mother.

But for every woman who'd inherited the Mother Wound and didn't know she could break it.

For every daughter told to forgive and forget.

For every mother trapped in a pattern she didn't create.

For every lineage severed from its own knowing.

I spoke aloud, to the universe, to the ancestors, to the women who would read this story someday:

"If you're carrying this wound—

"If your mother couldn't love you the way you needed—

"If she couldn't protect you the way she should have.

"If you've spent your whole life trying to earn what should have been given freely—

"It's not your fault.

There's nothing wrong with you.

"You are not too much.

"You are not too sensitive.

"You are not unlovable.

"You are not naïve.

"You inherited a distortion—

"A pattern.

"A wound that was installed long before you were born.

"And you can break it.

"Not by forgiving perfectly.

"Not by reconciling.

"Not by being 'spiritual enough' to rise above it.

"But by seeing it clearly.

"By naming it.

"By refusing to pass it forward.

"By choosing integration over inheritance.

"You can be the one who ends it.

"You can be the lightning that splits the tower.

"You can be the ancestor future daughters call on when they need strength and guidance.

"You are enough.

"You have always been enough.

"And the wound stops here.

"With you."

I sat back down at my altar.

Lit another candle.

And I made a final offering—a declaration.

Not to the ancestors this time.

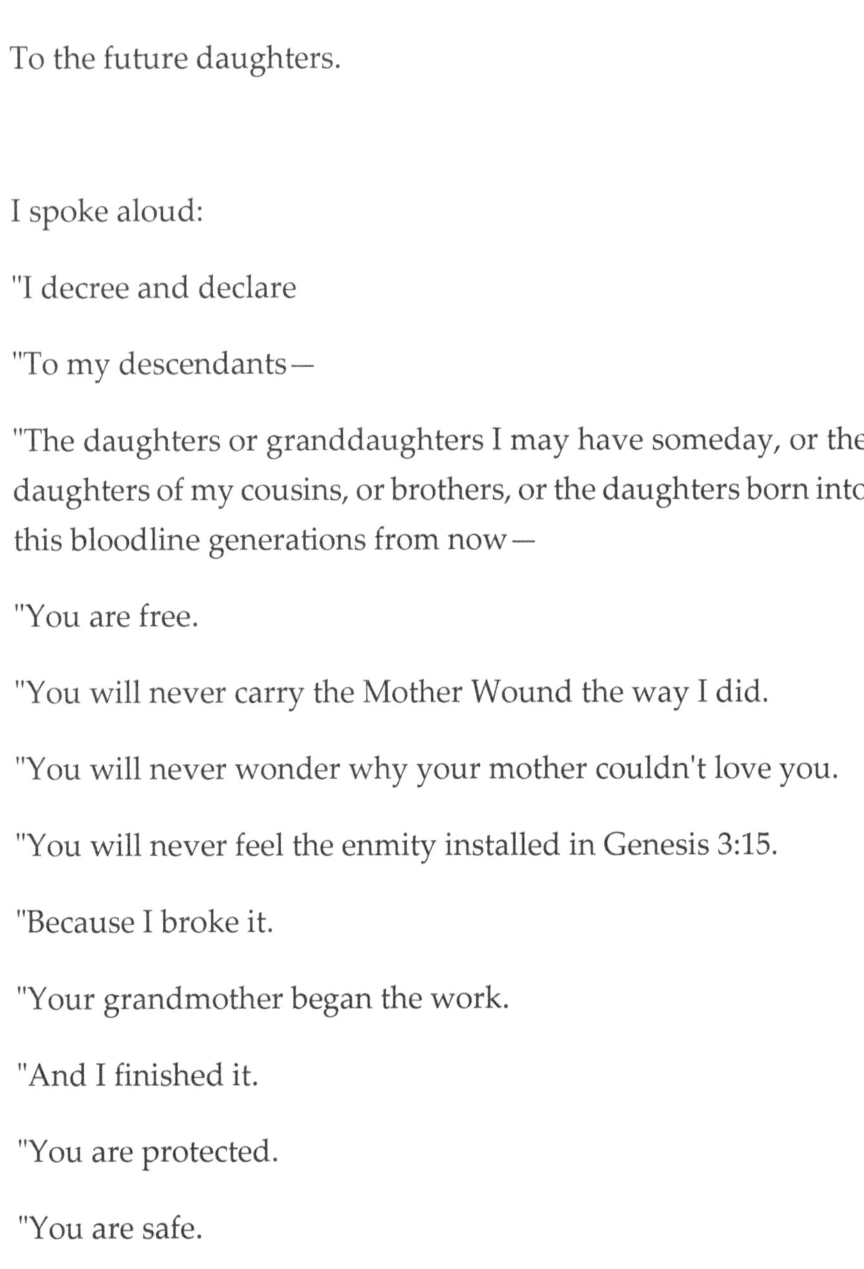

From me.

To the future daughters.

I spoke aloud:

"I decree and declare

"To my descendants—

"The daughters or granddaughters I may have someday, or the daughters of my cousins, or brothers, or the daughters born into this bloodline generations from now—

"You are free.

"You will never carry the Mother Wound the way I did.

"You will never wonder why your mother couldn't love you.

"You will never feel the enmity installed in Genesis 3:15.

"Because I broke it.

"Your grandmother began the work.

"And I finished it.

"You are protected.

"You are safe.

"You are loved—not conditionally, not with strings attached, but freely.

"And when you look back at your lineage, you will see:

"Yes, there was trauma and pain.

"Yes, there was wounding.

"But there was also a woman who said, 'No more.'

"A woman who stood in the fire and refused to let it consume her.

"A woman who broke the chains and set the captives free.

"That woman is me.

"And I did it for you—

For us.

"Live well and love freely.

"Know your worth.

"Take up all the space you were born to fill.

"And never, ever let anyone make you feel *adequate*.

"You are exactly enough.

"And you always have been."

I sat in the resonance of my words for a long time.

Feeling the weight of what I'd just spoken into existence.

The covenant I'd just made with the future.

And then I pulled one final card.

Not a question this time.

Just a closing.

A seal.

A confirmation that the work was complete.

Ace of Cups.

A new beginning.

Overflowing love.

Emotional fulfillment.

A chalice held by a hand emerging from the clouds, offering pure, unconditional love.

The kind of love I never got from my mother.

But the kind of love I finally learned to give myself.

I set the card on the altar.

And I whispered:

"It's done.

"The curse is broken.

"The Mother Wound ends here.

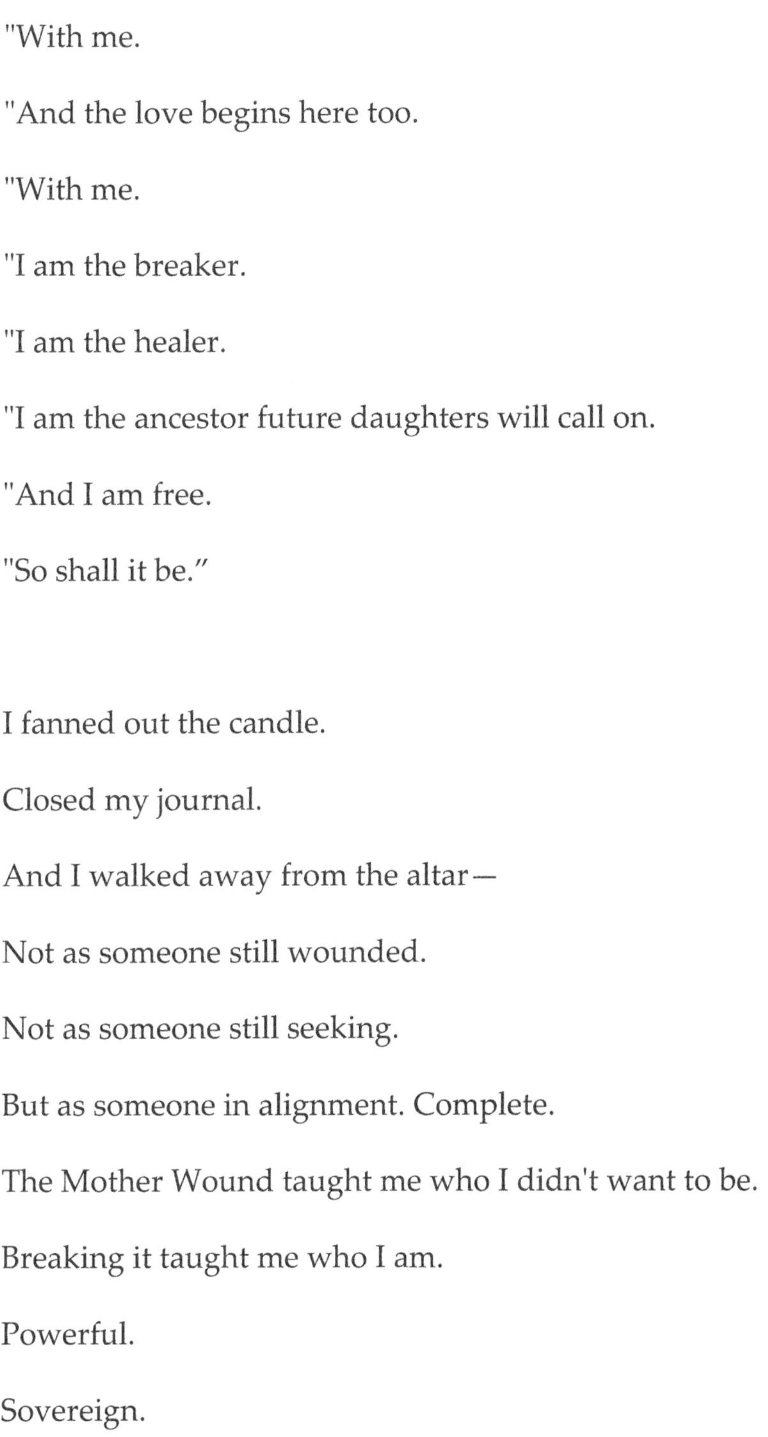

"With me.

"And the love begins here too.

"With me.

"I am the breaker.

"I am the healer.

"I am the ancestor future daughters will call on.

"And I am free.

"So shall it be."

I fanned out the candle.

Closed my journal.

And I walked away from the altar—

Not as someone still wounded.

Not as someone still seeking.

But as someone in alignment. Complete.

The Mother Wound taught me who I didn't want to be.

Breaking it taught me who I am.

Powerful.

Sovereign.

Whole.

Free.

If you have reached this point—know this: the Mother Wound is not abstract, and it is not harmless. Its tendrils run deep.

It determines how much you believe you deserve, what you will endure in the name of love, how you treat yourself, and how long you will abandon yourself to be chosen.

Left unhealed, it will repeat itself through your relationships, your identity, your body, your finances—even your children.

Naming it is not betrayal. Healing it is not disrespect. It is a disruption. And disruption is how a bloodline changes.

It is possible to break what's been passed down for generations—

I am proof.

And you can be too.

Place your hands on your heart. Feel the generations in your blood, the echoes of pain, the whispers of the women who came before.

"Remember who you are. "Call your name aloud.

"Let it vibrate through the lineages, through the walls of houses that have held too much silence.

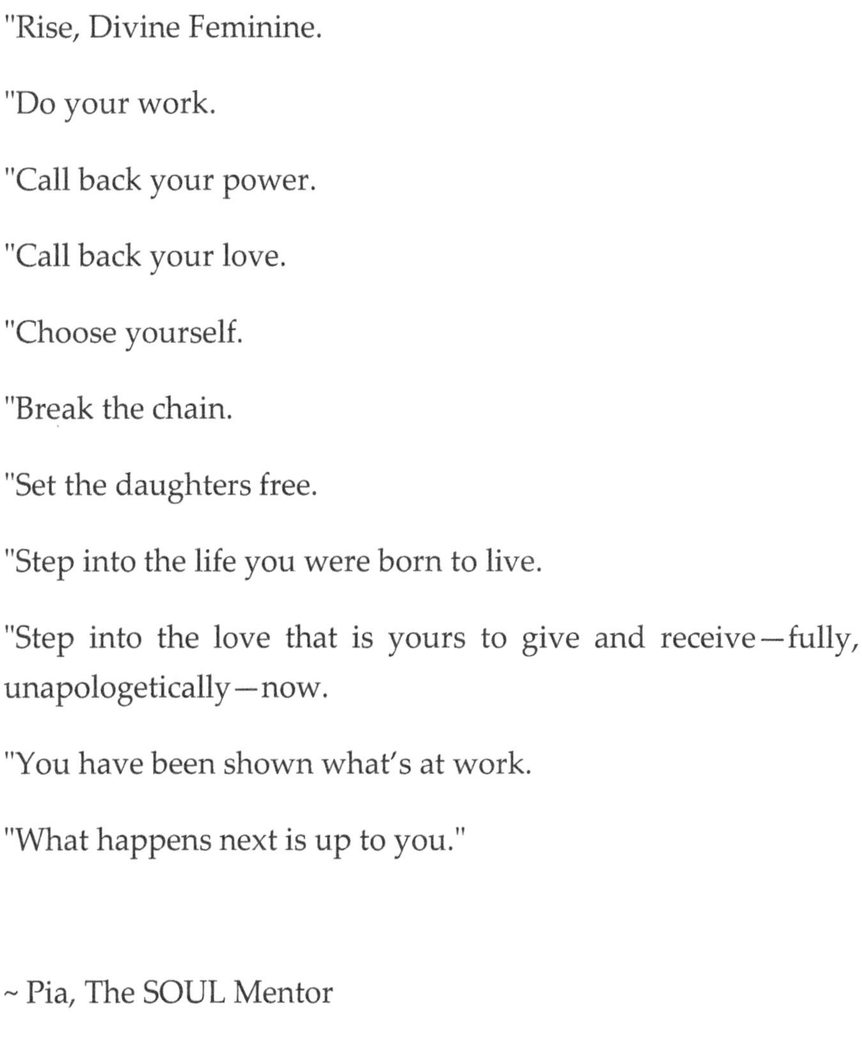

"Rise, Divine Feminine.

"Do your work.

"Call back your power.

"Call back your love.

"Choose yourself.

"Break the chain.

"Set the daughters free.

"Step into the life you were born to live.

"Step into the love that is yours to give and receive—fully, unapologetically—now.

"You have been shown what's at work.

"What happens next is up to you."

~ Pia, The SOUL Mentor

.

ABOUT THE AUTHOR

Pia is a certified hypnotherapist, past life regressionist, author, and founder of The SOUL Spa LLC and SOUL Spa Hypno®, where she guides individuals through deep soul work, ancestral healing, and past life regression. With a background in public health and over 20 years of experience counseling and mentoring women through emotional, spiritual, and generational trauma, her work sits at the intersection of psychology, hypnotherapy, practical spirituality, and soul healing.

She is known for helping clients identify inherited wounds—especially those rooted in maternal lineage—and for challenging spiritual narratives that prioritize forgiveness over understanding. Her approach does not bypass pain; it interrogates it. Not to dwell there, but to end cycles that have been repeating for generations.

This book was born from her own lived experience, her professional practice, and the countless stories of women who came to her asking the same unspoken question: Why does this keep happening in my bloodline?

Pia believes that some souls enter families not as descendants, but as disruptors—here to interrupt patterns, expose contracts made in fear, and restore choice where there was once obligation.

She lives and works in Georgia as a mentor, practitioner, and spiritual advisor for those ready to transform their lives, stop surviving their inheritance and start rewriting it.

If this book activated something in your soul and you feel called to explore your own journey, scan the code below to learn about hypnotherapy, past life regression sessions, training opportunities, and more.

Soulspahypno.com

www.ingramcontent.com/pod-product-compliance
Ingram Content Group UK Ltd.
Pitfield, Milton Keynes, MK11 3LW, UK
UKHW022026190726
13853UKWH00005B/2127

9 798234 006066